PRAISE FOR MASTERING THE GOOD LIFE

Astrid V.J.
USA Today bestselling author and DreamBuilder™ coach

Mastering the Good Life is a unique self-help book. In comparison to many others I've read that show you the door, this is quite clearly the key! Robb Whitewood synthesizes all the knowledge, skills and tools required for an individual to unlock the door into a life you love living. This book is beautifully written and presented succinctly in a style that is easy to follow and in a sequence that makes applying the principles easy.

If you're like Alice, stuck in a room where your oversized tears become the river that will ultimately drown you, read this book. Let it be the key. For you, too, can live in Wonderland!

Owen Power
Chronically depressed since my late twenties, searching for meaning in my life

As someone who tragically viewed fulfilment as a distant dream, *Mastering the Good Life* shook my misconceptions to their core. Robb's irreproachable guidance seamlessly opened my mind to the fact that healing, wholeness and a life of deep-rooted happiness was truly mine for the taking.

Richard Odey

Having a long-term relationship challenge with my wife, wondering if we'll ever love each other again

I have read many self-development and motivational books, but *Mastering the Good Life* is in a special class of its own. This is because the book is based on real, hard-won experiences rather than on distant research and vague statistics. *Mastering the Good Life* is a result of personal as well as oriental knowledge and spoke to me from the very first page.

What made me believe in the content of this book is the way Allison herself has healed and moved on after Robb's unexpected and painful passing. The courage Allison has exhibited publishing this inspiring book is truly incredible.

I was someone who lived a life of great expectations, expecting people to act or treat me in certain ways, and I got hurt in the process. I have come to realise in this book that people are different and have their different perspectives about life, and so I now respect each person's worldview. I chose to let myself heal because the only thing I really have is me.

I particularly enjoyed the Seven Hearts exercise. It was an eye-opener that has helped me improve the quality of the relationship with my wife. However, I love this book most for its mental and practical exercises. The stress-relieving exercises in this book work magic.

I recommend *Mastering the Good Life* to anyone who is in search of true happiness and a sustainable change. If you are willing to put in the required effort to change, *Mastering the Good Life* is the amazing blueprint you need.

Yvonne Bowen

Feeling alone and unsupported by family and friends, deeply unhappy

An engaging, transformative book I seriously didn't know I needed. Robb Whitewood acts as a guide and navigator in *Mastering the Good Life*, providing you with tools and evidence-based strategies to captain your way into a more fulfilling life. From his touching narrative to his experience as a master NLP trainer and hypnotherapist, Robb and Allison's comforting words act as a guiding light that truly makes this book a work of infinite wisdom that you'll want to keep coming back to.

Gemma Scholl

Burnt out from the corporate rat race, looking to find myself

I've had the privilege to work with Robb and Allison during a turbulent time where I felt lost in life. The principles in this book are a summary of some of the key techniques that helped empower me to make positive choices for my life. I was able to focus on what mattered to me and what made me happy. I now am living the life I have chosen and am feeling truly fulfilled. These tools and strategies do work – I am proof of it! This book is a must-read for anyone who is feeling a little lost or jaded.

Andrew Wong

String of failed relationships, feeling defective and unproductive in life

Mastering the Good Life is a book you'll want to keep referring to, in the way you might turn to a close friend for advice. Whitewood and Low take their readers on an incisive journey through their own minds, teaching them to navigate their own perception. The writing is warm and funny, but above all it provides clear, useful strategies for any person dissatisfied with their life. Through reading this book, you can become a captain at the helm of your life, rather than letting the waves push you around.

Mira Loukesh
Self-development junkie looking for a long-lasting transformation

I've always enjoyed personal development. I feel like I have done all the courses and read all the books! I've got to say that I am living my dream life – I have a great family and kids and live in a beautiful house. Continuous personal development is a must for me; when you get complacent, things can change pretty quickly. *Mastering the Good Life* is a necessary book in your personal development toolkit. The tools provided are useful and can be done by anyone, anywhere to gain instant results. I loved the exercises on the vagus nerve reset – I have never seen that anywhere else before. I also loved the relationships section and exercises. I know this is a book that I will return to time and time again.

MASTERING
the good life

Principles for creating fulfilment and freedom

Robb Whitewood with Allison Low

Mastering the Good Life: Principles for Creating Fulfilment and Freedom
Robb Whitewood with Allison Low

Copyright © 2021 by Allison Low. All rights reserved.

This book or any portion thereof may not be reproduced or used in any manner whatsoever without the express written permission of the publisher, except for the use of brief quotations in a book review.

Editor: Bryony Sutherland
Cover concept: Allison Low
Cover design: The Scaly Merchant
First printed edition (2021) in Australia by: McPherson's Printing Group

 A catalogue record for this book is available from the National Library of Australia

ISBN 978-0-6452202-0-9 (paperback)
ISBN 978-0-6452202-3-0 (hardback)
ISBN 978-0-6452202-6-1 (colour hardback)
ISBN 978-0-6452202-1-6 (kindle)
ISBN 978-0-6452202-4-7 (Adobe PDF)

Also by Robb Whitewood:
Untraditional Hsing-I: Secret of Five Element Boxing
(Paladin Press, 1999)

DEDICATION

Robb's dedication

I dedicate this book to the finest human I have ever known. Without her I would not have known what love was. Thank you to my girl, Allison.

Allison's dedication

I dedicate this book to every truth-seeking warrior on an inward quest to create an authentic life.

Our dedication

Together we dedicate this book to all our treasured students and clients who have been courageous seekers of fulfilment. You have been our greatest teachers.

A PERSONAL NOTE FROM ALLISON LOW

For a year I debated whether to tell you at the beginning or the end of this book about Robb Whitewood's unexpected and sudden passing. As I write this, the grief is still holding an honourable space even after four years of losing him.

On the evening of the thirtieth of March 2017, I entered through the front door of our home with worry on my shoulders and fear in my heart. Over the past few hours several text messages and phone calls to Robb had gone uncharacteristically unanswered. The absence of energy hit me like a cold wave as I moved through our home, looking for Robb. The kindred soulmate instinct told me Robb was not here anymore. Devastatingly, my instinct was right: Robb had passed on.

Thousands of our students and clients may pick up this book wondering how and why Robb died. They knew a stoic Robb who was rarely sick, and who could kill with his martial-arts trained hands. The other side to Robb was extremely sensitive. He chose a Chihuahua for his pet dog and would go gaga at the sight of a baby. Robb would give anyone a hug who wanted one. His hugs would reach your soul and the feeling you received was unconditional love.

Robb died from a berry aneurysm. In lay terms, there was a massive bleed from a blood vessel bursting on the left side of his brain. This is the only way Robb would have been happy going out; he never wanted to have lived with his brain or body debilitated in any way. Robb was a man of power and gentle persuasion. He lived to heal. If he couldn't do that, then he would believe he was no longer needed on this earth.

Robb was charismatic and strangers would crowd around him as if he were a guru bearing important messages that spoke to each person individually. He was an extreme introvert, yet a master on stage when speaking to thousands.

Out of loving fun, Robb and I would tease each other from time to time, and so now Robb isn't here to get me back, I'm going to spill some beans on him. His spirit would get a little laugh, I'm sure. At thirteen years old, Robb was a stage magician, performing up and down the east coast of Australia in clubs, pubs and shopping centres. I never really understood why he kept this a secret as I found it cool and fascinating. Robb and I were soulmates and I feel blessed and honoured to have spent many years by his side, having so many interesting adventures on a quest to heal the world. We were deeply in love and the best of friends.

At the time of Robb's passing, this book and a few others he was working on were not ready for publishing. In the days that followed his death, I made a decision to complete and publish his books posthumously. Robb and I were together for almost twelve years and I lived and breathed Robb's wisdom 24/7, so any content I've added is aligned with Robb's philosophies. This book is written in the first person, and our words represent one voice with unified messages. Robb would be fulfilled knowing that he can reach you through our words in this book to support you.

One of Robb's students so aptly described my late husband as an 'Earth Angel'. Robb's mission in life was to bring heaven to earth. He knew that if just one person could breathe easier because of his existence, he would have done his job. This job I know has now been done thousands and thousands of times over.

Rest easy, Robb, for now your students, your clients, and the readers of this book will carry on your mission. We are the ripples of love and wisdom.

CONTENTS

INTRO 1

HOW BEST TO USE THIS BOOK 9

PART I – WHAT BROUGHT YOU HERE 12

Chapter 1 – Why the droopy tree? 15

Chapter 2 – Your survival strategy is working perfectly 31

Chapter 3 – Who's in the driver's seat? 51

PART II – BUILDING SOLID FOUNDATIONS 74

Chapter 4 – The connected whole 77

Chapter 5 – You're on the path to fulfilment 83

Chapter 6 – You are not them 97

Chapter 7 – The real you 111

Chapter 8 – Instant influence 121

Chapter 9 – When transformation begins 131

PART III – TRANSFORMATION 144

Chapter 10 – The power of questions 147

Chapter 11 – Release it 153

Chapter 12 – Redefine it 171

Chapter 13 – Creating fulfilment 181

PART IV – RELATIONSHIPS REVOLUTION 196

Chapter 14 – Relationships are life 199

Chapter 15 – Relationship magic 213

Chapter 16 – The seven hearts 231

Chapter 17 – It's all about you 247

OUTRO 255
ACKNOWLEDGMENTS 261
LAST WORDS FROM THE AUTHORS 265
SUGGESTED READING AND VIEWING 267
ONLINE RESOURCE LINKS 269
ROBB'S BIO 271
ALLISON'S BIO 273

The content of this book is for informational purposes and is not intended as medical advice, or as a substitute for the medical treatment by a physician.

INTRO

Most humans are living life small. Like looking at an elephant through a microscope, they are never truly experiencing the magic of their whole world. The evidence of this lies in their perpetual pursuit of materialistic trophies that have become their happiness measurement stick. You've come here because you are not this, not in your heart. You are seeking genuine fulfilment that resonates with your true desires, and you won't stop searching until you find it. My mission is to help you find it.

Many of the personal empowerment organisations today teach a type of positive psychology that uses high-energy optimism and punchy positive affirmations to crowd out pain and fear. This approach creates a glossy veneer that peels off over a short time. If you attend these events, you recognise so many repeat attendees in the audience. Are they truly there to create internal change, or are they hooked on the adrenaline? This book is not that.

I'm going to take an experienced guess at why you've picked up this book. You're searching for answers to your challenges, discontentment, loneliness, feelings of restlessness, emptiness or suffering. These are symptoms of your needs not being met and your inability to express yourself. These symptoms have a root cause of inadequate communication strategies and a less than ideal value in your own best interests. You may be seeking the path to success and happiness. Whether you're here for the resolution of pain or the attainment of pleasure, the solution process is going to be the same.

Perhaps these sentiments resonate with you:

- 'I am here, but I want to be there'
- 'I am stuck, and don't know how to move forward'
- 'I have this, but I don't want it'
- 'I think this way, but I wish I didn't'
- 'I wish I was ____' or, 'I wish they were ____'

The beauty of the insights I'm going to share with you is that, no matter the problem, you can apply them to resolve any of your troubles.

Have you ever wondered how your history has led you to the very seat you are in right now? Everyone has an internal compass that navigates them through life. Your internal compass is adjusted by each of your experiences since birth. Our default settings are to safeguard survival; retain freedom; cultivate belonging; to love, be loved and to seek meaning and purpose in our lives. Would you like to learn how to adjust your internal compass, so it gets you back on your chosen path to realise your true desires?

I wrote this book to share with you a new framework through which to view life. It's about reclaiming space by removing fluff and distraction, and giving you room to create the experiences you truly value. It's about giving the stuck emotions a route out. It's about enriching your social life and attracting quality relationships. It's about becoming the creator of a fulfilling life. The by-product of the work we will do together is unconditional happiness.

In learning relationships, you either have a master and apprentice or a teacher and a student. At school, the teacher disseminates information. The student is then expected to regurgitate the information back to the teacher, one possible answer for each question. But life isn't like that, and nor is this book. Every question has many answers. My teaching paradigm encompasses learning concepts and methods that reward you with the new skills and insights to discover who you are and understand the dynamics of how you interface with the people and the world around you. It is from this deep understanding that you can affirm your unique true qualities and discover how you can transform and embrace a self-perpetuating fulfilment.

Firstly, let me be clear: If anyone starts telling you that this or that is the only true way to success or happiness, run away. There are as many answers to a puzzle as there are people to answer it. This would imply that the vast majority of what is taught in school is questionable. We are all unique, with the potential for brilliance if we only let ourselves be. Please understand, success is not a destination. Frequently you will hear people, maybe even yourself, say, 'When I get this new car or buy a house, I'll be happy' or, 'When I get this qualification or degree, I'll be successful.' Or how about, 'I'll be happy when I find a life partner, get married, have a baby'?

Happiness is a state of being; it has nothing to do with doing or having. Ironically, what I have observed over the years is that individuals that are masters at being happy generally end up with great stuff, while those who chase material possessions don't necessarily lead happy lives.

You may be asking who is Robb Whitewood and what makes him such an expert on mastering the good life? This is a reasonable question. I was born in Brisbane, Australia in August 1960. My parents were acrobats who travelled the world. This meant I spent many of my early years in a caravan or being dumped with people that resented having to look after me for up to a year at a time. How did I perceive those childhood years? Damaging, full of abandonment, physical and psychological abuse, fear and constant anxiety.

Putting my traumatic childhood history aside, I have enjoyed many colourful and diverse experiences. In 1980 I represented Australia in the International Games; a full-contact martial arts tournament. This was the precursor to Mixed Martial Arts (MMA). I represented Australia again in 1987 in the Wu Shu Games of China, as a competitor and coach. During this time, I was studying Traditional Chinese Medicine, specialising in Acupuncture. I trained for eight years in Australia, two years in Tokyo and one year in Taiwan. While in Japan I spent many of my mornings meditating and chanting within the shrine of a priest named Tojinja. Tojinja told me I was 'one of twelve'. He told me my life would not be my own. I was too young at the time to understand what he meant, and it would take me another twenty years to fully comprehend the meaning.

One of the best adventures I had was appearing as a stunt actor in a range of Australian commercials, movies and TV series. This was the direct result of a dare from a group of students from my training courses. They ganged up on me and voiced together, 'If what you teach is so good, how are you going to challenge your own personal boundaries?' Well, I thought getting into the TV and film industry would be a suitable challenge, as the line is long and the door is small to enter into this world.

These are the lowlights and highlights of my life as they come to mind. What does all of this mean? To me, it means that life is to be lived, the dark and the light. Fun is to be had. Life can only be spent, never saved. It is measured not by a bank balance but by the quality of the time we spend and the self-perpetuating fulfilment we enjoy.

It's important to embrace a reality where pain and challenge are all part of the process. I once had the privilege of spending a couple of hours with a world-ranked tennis player. As we spoke, he said something fascinating that I think many may not appreciate about competition. He said, 'You have to get used to losing.' At school we are taught winning is everything and losing is bad. But as a professional tennis player, you lose a lot. If you want to master anything in life; get used to losing quickly and embrace it as the only way forward. In my observations, successful people lose significantly more than their unsuccessful counterparts. This may be as high as a twenty loss to a single win. Average individuals focus on the first few losses and stop, while extraordinary people continue to focus on the win, regardless of the losses.

The way is the path —Lao Tzu

Simple questions, simple answers. At the beginning of a session with a new client, I ask a couple of questions such as: What mischief have you got yourself into? What is bothering you? What is the one question you could ask me, that if answered would solve your problem once and for all, today? Then, I sit back and listen. This is where I discover who a person is and the adventures they have been on. Their story unfolds with its depth and breadth and the meanings it has for them. It's also the means by which you come to understand why this person is in front of you at this moment.

Now, there will be as many stories as there are people with problems. I am frequently amazed at the expanse of mischief, distress, trouble, turmoil and downright silliness people can get themselves into. (By the way, I don't exclude myself from this human dilemma.) And what I have gathered over three decades of clinical experience and thousands of sessions is that there are only really three main themes to the issues people experience in life: relationships, health and finances.

Connected symptoms

Let me let you into a little secret. When I sit and listen to someone's story, I don't listen to the actual content. Instead, I listen for the process of the problem, looking for the connections between the symptoms and discovering a root core issue. Once this core issue is defined and dissolved, so will be all the connected symptoms. This is what I'll be teaching you in *Mastering the Good Life*: how to look into yourself, use your observational skills and follow the lines of self-enquiry that I'll lay out for you. In following the process you'll discover why you are here and not over there where you want to be. Knowing how a problem was created allows you to dissolve it by transforming your thoughts, feelings and actions.

Shadow problems

Often individuals will present themselves to me with the desire to improve their financial situation. However, as we sit and talk, it becomes clear that their relationships present the area in need of attention. It's amazing to recognise how a small improvement in one area can have a significant impact on another without any direct work on that area. So, although financial troubles may be the presenting problem, a relationship issue may be quickly identified as the shadow problem, the real cause for the imbalance.

Most of your issues, blocks and challenges are inter-related. Like a domino effect, once you resolve or address one area, other issues magically disappear without actively addressing them! You will know when an issue is one of those 'secondary' or 'symptomatic' issues when it dissolves automatically as you work through this book, focussing on other issues. One of the by-products of real change is a type of amnesia regarding your original problem. Often it will take a friend or family member to notice the change in you, which can be surprising if you no longer retain the feelings or behaviours of your former problem.

Uncovering a problem covered by another problem

Another phenomenon that is common is that once an issue is resolved, another issue can pop up that you weren't conscious of before. It's like when your headache lifts, you start to recognise your aching tooth! Your tooth was always aching, but your headache was covering the toothache. Often a problem that may have been obvious in the past has over time become 'accepted' and settled in as your new normal. It's only when we poke around a bit and the Band-Aid is lifted that this problem returns to the fore.

Another type of problem can be like a knife in your back, but you're choosing to focus on the splinter in your finger. You are in a violent domestic relationship but your focus is the rising price of vegetables.

In joining me on this adventure, the first thing to understand is that change can only happen if you are open to the possibility that you may be right or you may be wrong. Ultimately, your ongoing position needs to be that your viewpoint today may become obsolete in the future, and you may be required to let go of what you historically believed. Answers to challenges were not known to you before because your perception was closed off to the area where the solution is found. In widening your perception and taking on new skills to see the once unseeable, your awareness automatically expands. With your learning hat on, your nervous system is activated, your attention is sparked, your positive emotions start flowing and change can be immediate.

The change I encourage is one that is naturally aligned with you. Your natural potential is cloaked with layers of self-doubt, societal conditioning, parental expectations and your ancestral memories. I will help you navigate safely through these layers. Change occurs by shifting previously rigid thought patterns and opening up a smorgasbord of options inviting new decisions that flow to new behaviours and improved outcomes.

Relax, and the rest will come together. My dream is for you to read this book and live a life that is meaningful, loving, creative and perceptually long!

HOW BEST TO USE THIS BOOK

Imagine reading this book is like embarking on the creation of a self-sustaining property. You are building your dream house on a fertile piece of land that provides an abundance of food to feed yourself and your loved ones. You recognise there is a plan that is to be followed in a particular order to ensure the best possible outcome. You sort through and weigh up your thoughts and desires, then you step through the process from building solid foundations to moving through each stage of the development, using the right tools, techniques, skills and support. Each aspect of the development has value and purpose. From time to time, you stand back to admire the transformation unfolding. You understand that throughout the entire journey, the level of success of each part of the project is determined by the quality of the relationships between them, and you appreciate the magnificence of flow when all parts are in alignment with each other. At the completion of your mission, you behold a self-perpetuating, self-fulfilling creation.

In exactly the same way, this book is presented in a prescriptive order that will give you the most successful self-fulfilling outcomes.

It may be tempting to cherry-pick information that appears instantly compelling or scoop sections where you may have spied some possible quick answers for your situation. However, without the foundational work, the end result will be deficient. I've weaved subtle metaphors that span the length of the book. So, if you're a person that likes to take shortcuts, keep an eye out for the section that describes this behavioural inclination and some of the related drawbacks in the realisation of fulfilment.

I would heartily encourage you to reread this book, again, in its entirety, at any time you feel induced to. Life is a moving story, where new puzzles appear as a result of new events, new circumstances or relationship bumps. These puzzles are opportunities for you to grow again and add to your skills toolkit for mastering the good life.

Exit, breathe, reset

At times you might become emotionally overwhelmed. Below are two options for you to address this state, if it arises.

1. Break state

Look around the room, notice the colour and textures of the walls and decide whether they are different to the ceiling. Remember what you had for breakfast, check the weather outside and take three deep slow breaths. This is called a 'break state', and it allows you to interrupt the emotional release. Do a practise run of this now.

2. Somatic experiencing

Suspend all thoughts, feel your way through the emotion, focus on the feelings and notice where they are in your body. Stay with the feelings until they subside.

PART I

What brought you here

I'M WONDERING WHAT BROUGHT you here. If you are like one of my students or clients, then I'd take an experienced guess that you're looking for answers rather than entertainment. My highest intention for you is to find what you are looking for with ease, grace and a touch of humour.

When a tree is drooping, losing its leaves and not producing fruit, we look at the soil, the stuff the roots are feeding from to keep it alive and thriving. We first need to identify whether the soil has parasites, whether it has life-giving nutrition, whether it has the right amount of water. When a tree is nourished from within, the warmth and light from the sun catalyses flourishing. You are no different to a tree in this respect. Some gentle and strategic unearthing is required to discover what has been out of sight for a long time. Assessing what is going on underneath will give you the insights so you can take conscious action in the right way. A mistake would be to just guess and throw everything at the soil in the hope it solves the issue.

It's time to put on your curiosity hat, as I show you how you got to where you are today and why your stuff has been persisting up until now. You'll appreciate what conditions you've placed on yourself, a self-imposed box. Understanding the unique drivers of your thoughts, feelings and behaviour will give you the pivot points for building new foundations.

CHAPTER 1

WHY THE DROOPY TREE?

I don't like what's in my sandwich

> Joe has lunch with the same co-workers each day at work. Each lunch time he opens his lunch box and there is a deep inward breath followed by a slow sigh and an annoyed utterance, 'Not peanut butter sandwiches again.' After months of Joe's lunchtime ritual, Brian, a colleague sitting opposite finally remarks, 'Joe, ask your wife to make you a different type of sandwich!' To which Joe replies, 'I'm not married, I make my own sandwiches.'

The vast majority of people complain about the life they live, not realising that each day they make their own sandwiches. The habit of making the same sandwich becomes comfortable and predictable, but are you satisfied? Are you fulfilled? Would you like more than a bread-and-butter life?

The first rule

The first rule is, there are no rules. I will share concepts and guidelines and teach you how to make inquiries about your thoughts, feelings and behaviours to expand your self-awareness. Insights are the pivotal point to powerful and rapid transformation.

I recall the first lines of the *Tao Te Ching*: 'The way that can be spoken is not the constant way.' Any time you say a thing is one way, there will be a person or situation to counter it. Similarly, the ten commandments are invariably open to interpretation. The main reason for this is that they are written in an absolute form, however, nothing is perfect or absolute. Thou shall not kill does not seem to include chickens, cows or fish. If that's the case, I'm going to hell for sure, not for the fish, but for the chickens. It seems to be acceptable to kill when you are defending your country. It seems acceptable to kill your attacker when they are trying to kill you.

Rather than absolutes, here we will work through a series of concepts, such as having an objective and going with your natural flow until it is reached; or, that which you resist, persists; or, that you can only see a quality in another person that already exists within you. Throughout the book I'll be presenting the idea that your actions or inactions lead to consequences, outcomes and results; there is no such thing as right or wrong, good or bad.

An idea that I fell in love with many years ago as a student of martial arts was the notion of grace rather than force. Grace is as effective as the single bullet at the right moment to stop the enemy leader in their tracks. It is about finding and developing elegant strategies to improve relationships. It is effective, time and resource efficient, and requires the ability to develop empathy for the task at hand. It is one of the cornerstones of mastery. One of the most amazing benefits of grace is that the small can overcome the mighty: size, strength, position and power all become irrelevant.

The assassin

> Batu, a Japanese warlord, heard on the grapevine that another warlord had engaged an assassin to kill him. He questioned his staff to find out who the assassin could be. Try as he might, he could not find the assassin. As he was walking the grounds of his garden, he felt the sudden sharp pain of steel penetrating his body. As he lay there dying, the one person he hadn't question was standing over him, knife in hand. In total disbelief, the warlord looked at this man who had been a trusted servant and gardener for his family since he was five years old. For the last forty-five years this man had worked in the garden, producing beauty and harmony.

What Batu failed to realise was that the gardener had always been employed by the other warlord. To Batu's detriment, he did not question the gardener because he was beyond question.

A lot of the thoughts, behaviours and problems that we have are just that; they are beyond question. Our perception of our happiness or sadness and our self-image of who and what we are, are frequently the gardener in the system: they are beyond question. How much happiness do we expect? What do we think of the world? Is it a good place or a bad place? Where do you perceive you fit into society in terms of your self-esteem; are you at the top or at the bottom? Questioning the unquestionable will shine a light on areas you can modify to change an event and remove perpetuating causes of a problem.

What is a problem, anyway?

When your life is not going well, or in the way you expect it to, this can bring about feelings of futility, unrest, stress, frustration, anger and even depression. Maybe you perceive you attract more than your fair share of 'oh bugger' moments. Often many of my clients see me because they don't know how or why things are going wrong, but they know they don't feel happy and they definitely don't feel fulfilled. A good portion of my clients come to visit me because they feel lonely, lost and disheartened. Often they have lost their spark.

When you're not doing the things you love to do, and you can't seem to allow yourself to do them, you lose the will to get out of bed, and lack the motivation to do anything. When you are marching to the beat of someone else's drum, you feel resentful. When any of your significant relationships are in conflict, you may feel sad, confused or betrayed. Whether you are struggling with your finances, your health or with your relationships, the unrelenting anxiety triggered just by thinking about your problem is the real thief of a fulfilling life. When you fixate on an unknown, an uncertainty, it's the impatience to know it all right now that becomes the problem. Being afraid that you might be stuck forever like this adds another layer. What do you keep telling yourself about being stuck?

In the art of living, we cannot avoid challenging situations. A problem is a problem because it is experienced as such. It has become intrusive, overwhelming, debilitating, hopeless, life zapping. Yet another layer occurs when you believe this situation, event or conflict shouldn't be happening. Someone else standing in your shoes may not perceive this same thing as a problem. The intricate combination of you and how you interface with your outside world is what has created this reality for you.

We each have our unique blind spots. I expect you've come to read this book because you are searching for a resolution or at the very least to find your mojo and get back in the groove of enjoying life. Right now you are a step ahead: you're reading this book because you're curious and open to receive what is about to come.

You may have a problem list. You've sorted the problems in a priority order. At the top is the most important one. Your list heading is: *What's my blind spot?* Your by-line is: *Please help me out*. You may already have a preconceived idea of what is causing this. Often, we fall into the trap of assigning the wrong cause to a problem as it's the most convenient self-protecting reason you are able to latch on to.

You are not broken, so there will be no fixing required. You are not your problem, and your problem is not you. What we will work on together is releasing redundant beliefs and establishing new thought patterns so you can acquire new behaviours. In the trip we are about to take, you are always the captain. I am the navigator.

I have no doubt that this relationship issue, health challenge, or financial problem that is at the top of your list certainly goes on between your left and right ear; your top six inches. The repetitive thoughts and the emotional loading that goes with your problem might keep you awake at night, you may seek out soothing through eating quick carbs, boozing it up, burying yourself in work, checking your emails for the tenth time in two hours, scrolling aimlessly through your social media feed, going out for your third coffee today, acting out on those close to you, blaming and shaming others. Or maybe you are in denial and can't see any of the distraction stuff you do.

Often avoiding the real issue creates a secondary layer to your original problem. When you start thinking about your problem, you might feel so overwhelmed you enter your distraction mode, seamlessly. Sometimes you simply ignore it. You may have given up on trying to resolve it, but deep down it bugs you. It's there in the background and it's not going away. You may have become a master of misdirecting others away from seeing your problem, or you may deny it's a problem at all. Ultimately, you would like to sort it out and you know you can feel better about your life.

How much a problem creates suffering is directly linked with how much it threatens your survival, be that real or perceptional. I have observed in every one of my clients that the survival threat is founded in a perceptional distortion; either in the perception that their problem is a life-and-death matter, or a faulty perception where the elements holding the perception up remained unchallenged or unresolved. Yet every one of my clients survived their problem. So, when a problem presents, it is important to remove the faulty perceptional factors, so you can fully understand the reality of your situation. Making decisions from this position puts you on a level playing field.

You may have attached yourself to an outcome that you never seem to reach and, as a result of that perpetual reaching and striving, you've missed some of life's real gems. It's time to discover whether that unachievable outcome is really of value to you or whether there is another way. Perhaps there is an alternate outcome that is just as appealing. This is about seeing the possibilities. Ask yourself this: Is this my problem or someone else's problem? Often, we take on others' problems and in doing so have no control to initiate and direct change.

> How do you catch a wild monkey in the jungle? Place an orange inside a jar and tie the jar to a tree. The opening of the jar must be large enough for the monkey to get his hand in, but small enough that he cannot get it out once he grabs the orange. The monkey does not let go of the orange even

> though his freedom depends on it and it is a matter of life and death.

How long do you hold on to your orange, knowing that it is impossible to retrieve it using the method you are using and all the while, your freedom is being taken away? If you are blinded by the obsession with getting the orange, you cannot see the trap. How long will the futility of your behaviour of not letting go lead you into trouble? By focussing only on the orange, what are you missing out on, what opportunities have passed you by? How much energy and effort could be redirected into solving the puzzle differently or looking for another source of food? Maybe you don't even like oranges! What is the worst that can happen if you let go? What are the possibilities that appear when you let go? Persistence is a wonderful quality when you know when it's time to let go, time to pause and provide a space for yourself to assess. More courageous than holding on is the act of surrender.

Defining your dissatisfaction or problem

In a simple short sentence, clearly and concisely state your problem. If you have more than one, use the problem that is at the top of your list.

Equally important to knowing how to describe it, is knowing the parameters of the problem. Let's examine this further by using this set of questions.

- Is your problem conditional on a particular circumstance?
- Is your problem conditional on a particular relationship or with one particular person?

- Is your problem age related? What if you were five years old? What if you were one hundred years old? Would it still matter?
- What if you were the opposite gender, would it still be relevant?
- In what context or circumstance would this no longer be a problem?
- Would your problem still be valid last year, or ten years ago? How about twenty years into the future?

By answering these edge-finding questions you might now see that your problem is contained. Have you allowed a problem to spill over into the other parts of a reasonably otherwise okay life? How much laser focus do you have on this one problem, on this one area of your life? How much time do you spend retelling the story of your problem without the premise of seeking a real solution? How open are you to solving your problem?

The following exercise will help you define your problem with sense cues. Sense cues are the way in which your brain encodes information. The questions in the exercise may seem strange. Remember we are not looking for logic here; we are bringing forth the language of your unconscious mind.

Transform a problem exercise

Grab a piece of paper and a pen. Write down the first answer to pop into your mind for each of these questions.

- What colour is your problem?
- What shape is it?
- Does it have a smell?
- Is there a texture to it?
- Now use just one word to describe your problem.

Take ten seconds to check the colour of the ceiling. (Remember the break state from earlier? This allows your brain to reset in readiness for the next part of the exercise.) Now, as quickly as you can, assign:

- a new colour
- a new shape
- a new smell
- a new texture

Using humour, rename your problem. The more absurd the better. If you're not feeling that creative, use Unicorn. From this point forward you'll refer to your problem with its new name.

All problems by their very nature are perceptional

Did that statement surprise you? It might seem like I'm not taking you seriously. I get it, your unicorn is not easy to tame because if it was, you'd already have done so by now, right? The thing is, taming your unicorn needs some insights into how to tame a unicorn. I guarantee we will work seriously on this together. For now, just put Unicorn in the back seat as I navigate you through the process of unpacking why we humans do the things we do and why we think the things we think. If you understand how problems are put together, it is much easier to reduce them down to a grain of sand. I often call problems puzzles because puzzles have solutions. Puzzles take you on an adventure that teaches you new skills and wisdom during the process of working them out.

Often when you are stuck in the middle of a problem, a fear can rise up in you from thinking this problem won't ever release. This fear state prevents you from embracing the solutions flowing past you every second. An imagined pain is never as bad as the pain of not moving into a place of empowerment through choice and action. How do you take off your Band-Aids? Quickly or painstakingly slowly? In reality, nothing ever remains constant. In releasing your tight grip on your perception, circumstances can transition, and your feelings will evolve. Tomorrow is brand new. Allow yourself to seize the opportunity in the next moment.

I'm not just going to show you how to solve your unique and special problem; I'm going to show you what creates your problem – any problem. The question for you to answer at the end of this part of the book is: 'How does changing your perception change your reality?'

The Australian Featherweight Champion family

I've mentioned already that my childhood memories involved being abandoned. As entertainers, my parents travelled constantly. The first time they left me, I was three or four years old and they went away for six months. When I was about seven or eight, they went away for over a year. This time, they left me with people who didn't really like me. It was a family of mostly boys. The second eldest of the boys became the featherweight boxing champion of Australia. The third eldest also became a featherweight boxing champion and the fourth eldest wanted to be featherweight champion. My problem was that they terrified me. If it wasn't physical, it was psychological abuse. Because I was an outsider invading their family, they were bound to attack. I had no social position within the group, which meant that in terms of the hierarchy, I was at the bottom. I was the smallest and the youngest. As a kid, I used to wonder what the hell I did wrong. I had lost my real family and was dumped into what for me was purgatory.

> **Failure and disappointment are the hammers and fire that harden the steel.**

This all had a major effect on my psychology and behaviour. I became traumatised and so many parts of my life became broken. I can tell you this story of my childhood now without a pang of emotion. It no longer affects me. If you were able to see my face as I was telling you this story, you would see that I have no emotional attachments associated with it; it's just a neutral memory. If you haven't resolved a painful, historical event, telling its story can have more emotional loading than the memory itself. It is not happening at this precise moment in time. I know it is just a memory with the gaps filled in: a fantasy.

I healed myself using the processes I'll be sharing with you. You may have no recollection of anything negative in your childhood. However, everything in your history that has happened has brought you to the seat you're sitting in right now. Childhood events bear the most weight on your behaviour, your beliefs, your decisions. You don't have to suffer a childhood trauma to be experiencing relationship, health or financial woes today. No one's childhood creates a perfect smooth-sailing life. Your parents and caregivers likely did the best they could with the knowledge and resources they had. You've done your best to get to where you are today. Life is nothing short of a miracle. We aren't going to be making you relive childhood, nothing like that. You'll be shaking off the things that you once thought were part of you and your identity. You'll soon discover that releasing all the baggage that is not serving you well will breathe new possibilities into your life. It's a personal evolution within a number of hours.

The beauty of my childhood experience of physical abuse is that, as a result, I learned how to fight and protect myself. I became involved in cage fighting before they had rules. If you know anything about this sport, you will know how tough it is. What I was really trying to do was kill a monster that lived inside my head. As far as methodologies go for killing internal monsters, that was the hard way. If you look at my face and my hands, you can see the scars from those fights. My nose was broken many times, little fingers dislocated, and I have busted knuckles. I fought with opponents much bigger than myself, but the fight could never be won because the fight was never with them.

You may also have had a less than ideal history. The objective here is to revel in that history and turn the shit of the past into the fertiliser of the future. Literally grow something from it. You have learned something from your experiences. Make those learnings work for you rather than trying to run away and hide or fight invisible monsters. Use your experiences to become better, stronger and wiser, to be of assistance to yourself and to others. I can guarantee that you have your own story that you replay. It is no more or less than anyone else's, it is just your own. It is unique. There is nothing right and there is nothing wrong, but it is not real. It is equivalent to a fantasy. You definitely remember it, but is it happening where you are at this precise moment in time? I highly doubt it. You may be saying 'yes but, yes but' right now, but let me tell you: it is still a fantasy. I may come across as a bit of a bully with regards to this particular subject, simply because your future happiness is directly linked to your ability to grasp this particular concept. If this concept doesn't sit well with you, then I'm inviting you to be open to it, as it is going to give you a head start on what is to come. Can you think of at least one positive thing that has come out of a problem you've encountered in history?

> Three young girls were playing in the street. They all witnessed a cat running across the road and being hit by a car. The cat died instantly, and its remains were unrecognisable as it was flattened into the road. The first girl screamed, fell to the ground and looked away in horror, crying uncontrollably. The second girl ran over and poked it with a stick, curious as to what was inside the cat. The third girl ran after the car that had hit the cat to make the driver take responsibility.

Each girl observed the exact same event but will tell the story in three very different ways. In the future, they will recount the story in the context of how they perceived it. As time passes the story will be adjusted and modified as the clarity fades and the mind fills in the gaps. Which story is right? Which girl is right? All of them and none of them. It is purely perceptional: a fantasy. With each additional observer witnessing the accident, a different variation of the story would be told. The event will be assigned a different meaning. How does the event shape the future behaviour and beliefs of each observer based on the story they have recorded in their memory?

Strengthen the weakest link

Chains break at their weakest link. Discover what your weakest link is in the wheel of life and strengthen it. Spending time and energy improving that which you are weakest at will lead to corresponding and often exponential improvements in other aspects of your life. If you are a workaholic and never get enough rest, that is your weak link. Get more rest, meditate, contemplate and spend more time on your hobbies, then watch as your productivity at work improves significantly with less effort. If you are great at relationships and socialising but are having difficulty getting a job, spend more time and energy on discovering what your passion is, take an aptitude survey, educate yourself and develop your knowledge and skills accordingly. Then look for a job that excites you. You will find the quality of your health and social life will improve because your mindset will switch to joy and relaxation.

We spend a significant proportion of our life at work, so it's worthwhile focussing effort on securing a job you enjoy and that meets your desired criteria. Those who have greater job satisfaction spend far less on toys, distractions, drugs and alcohol. Balancing the wheel of life doesn't mean you must spend equal amounts of time on rest, hobbies, work and socialising. However, if you only spend a small proportion of your time on rest and hobbies and the remainder on work, your wheel will be likely be wobbly. Think of how you spend your time as a bucket that has two holes in the side of it, one located high up and one down low. Fixing the highest hole will be a waste of time as you will only ever be able to fill the bucket up to the level of the lowest hole. Fix the lowest hole, and you will be able to fill the bucket all the way to the high hole. Fixing the weakest point produces a much better return on investment.

Rest and sleep

Just like any other muscle in your body, your brain needs time to recuperate after prolonged periods in one particular activity. Professional athletes have to take regular breaks for their muscles to recover from lactic acid build-up and the associated muscle soreness. If I told you to go out and run a marathon today, depending on your fitness levels, you might get through it. What would happen if I told you to run another marathon the next day? Would your muscles be as effective? What if you had to then do it again, the day after that? You'd be lucky to get out of bed by that point. You would be so fatigued that moving would be excruciating and ineffective.

Your brain works the same way. When you carry out an activity, electrical and chemical signals fire off in the brain. If you keep doing the same thing over and over, your brain becomes fatigued. How often have you been working on something for a long period of time and then come up against a brick wall? What happens when you sleep on it, or, if you walk away, do something else and come back to it? It seems like you are viewing the work through fresh eyes. In truth, all that's happened is your brain has had time to recover and build its reserves. Simply going off and doing something else has a solid basis in neurology. Apparently, Einstein used to do this if he came up against a problem he struggled to solve. If you're having a relationship issue, go and do some office work, or take a walk, phone a friend, read a book. Simply carrying out a different activity can allow the overworked part of your mental real estate sufficient time to recover and subsequently find the solution.

Go slower, do less, be more present in each activity. Multi-tasking does not exist – it's purely perceptional if you believe you are doing many things at the same time when in reality you are chopping and changing activities. Your brain cannot focus on two things simultaneously.

The fastest way into being overwhelmed is to look at everything you have to do and bounce your mind from one to the next. The antidote to this is to pick one thing and focus on that. Then tick it off. Prioritise. Ask yourself if you are addicted to adrenaline. Maybe you have created perpetual pressure on yourself as that's the only thing that sparks you up and you need it like a caffeine hit. Having read this chapter, I challenge you to observe how you spend your week. Is it balanced? Notice if you tend to run yourself into the ground or take too many tasks on, which results in very little being achieved. Notice whether you spend large amounts of time partaking in distracting, empty activities such as scrolling through your social media feed.

CHAPTER 2

YOUR SURVIVAL STRATEGY IS WORKING PERFECTLY

Addictive behaviour and beach balls

We are all addicted to something: junk food, shopping, sugar, coffee, chocolate, partying, tobacco, drugs, alcohol, drama, sex, social media, online games, over-working, adrenaline, complaining, being angry or frustrated, worrying, being stressed, being right, being dominant, gambling, talking incessantly, being depressed, being highly strung and being on the go all the time, doing, doing, doing! And breathe. The stuff we are addicted to can be identified as those things we seek out to give us a dopamine hit.

An addiction is not a problem until it becomes a problem. When it affects what you want to be and where you want to go in life. If you are aiming to clean up your addictions, then finding what drives the addictive behaviour is key. I have never observed in any of my addicted clients that they were a victim to a substance. The substance or activity overuse was always a Band-Aid, not the actual root problem. So many clients searching for a solution tell me when they first meet me that they are addicted, and they just want me to hypnotise them into stopping it. I tell them that's easily done but ask them what they will pick up next as their vice, their sedative, their emotional relief. So, we go on a voyage of discovery and resolve the root cause driving the addictive behaviour. It doesn't matter how big the ball of emotion is – the process is the same.

Generally, there will be an intense emotion that you do not like and that causes you to reach for something to dampen its effect. This is self-soothing, a type of self-medication. The root cause of most addictions is fear. Being afraid you're going to die, you're not worthy, you're not going to make it to some expected outcome. These emotional pangs are exactly what you are trying to run from when you form an addiction. These pangs are the fuel that stokes the flames of addiction.

Often the pangs are what you can mistakenly think is the addiction itself. The reason why you form this idea is because you have associated the 'medication' with the pang repeatedly and your body and mind can no longer tell the difference between the emotional pang and the 'medication' craving. Also, the uncomfortable emotions can be so hidden that you're not consciously aware of them, but you are fully aware of the 'medication', so you blame that. Often clients who use tobacco as their 'medication' tell me they are chemically addicted to it. I tell them sure, maybe you're right. But I wonder why is it they can sleep the whole night without a single puff. A whole six to ten hours without a single hit. The same goes for any of the other 'medications'. Sure, after repeated exposure to the substance or activity, neural networks and peptide receptors will have established. So yes, the sooner you resolve the root cause, the easier it will be.

When you experience the pang, you feel uncomfortable or threatened. Consequently, you look for a barrier that you can place between you. The pangs often show up when you slow your mind down. When there is an opening, a space in your day, when you are free of doing, you will observe yourself quickly filling in that space with another activity, just so you become distracted and don't have to feel the feelings bubbling under the surface. Yes, watching TV or streamed online programs is a doing activity.

During the ongoing global social isolation regulation of Covid-19, many of the usual distractions of everyday life are being removed and we can observe increased anxiety and other mental health issues, including a spike in suicides. Alcohol sales are booming during lockdowns and a lot of couch-shaped backsides are emerging. Not surprisingly, the number of marriage and partnership breakdowns are continuing to increase.

Imagine being at the beach with a beach ball and you have to keep it under the water. Unfortunately, every time you look at the beach ball, it gets bigger, but it *must* stay under the water because a fear of death comes up if it appears at the surface. When the weather is nice and calm, it is easy to keep the ball under the water. Hell, you can even do it with one hand and live life with the other. But the moment you are bored, stressed, under pressure or sick, the wind comes up, the waves grow bigger and it's all hands on this rotten beach ball to try and keep it under the water. And it's at this point you might participate in addictive or self-destructive behaviour.

The interesting thing is that, while you engage in those addictive behaviours, the metaphorical beach ball continues to expand, and you're not able to pop the ball because there is a neural boundary in place, protecting it. The nature of the distraction then has to be larger and larger to keep those unwanted feelings in the beach ball under control because the neural real estate has grown. Can you relate? Most people have been there or maybe you are there right now. Sometimes the subject of depression comes into this. As the ball gets bigger, you may be consumed by depression so that you do not have to deal with the feelings bubbling away inside.

You can work hard whilst finding new and stronger distractions to keep those growing beach balls under the water. Of course, the easiest thing to do would be to just get rid of the beach ball so that you can swim freely. All of a sudden, your friends would be commenting on how relaxed you looked, and how much you had achieved with minimal effort, all while remaining happy.

There is one last addictive behaviour that often slips under the radar. Intellectualising problems, understanding them in principle, but not doing the practical work to solve them. What does this look like? Incessant buying of personal development books but either leaving them unread, or failing to take action on anything presented within their pages. Or taking a never-ending stream of personal development courses without ever integrating any of the transformational teachings into your life. The fear of change can sometimes be greater than choosing to keep your problem. So, ask yourself, and answer if you can now: Why do I choose to hold on to my problem? Is it time to let go now?

Easy-hard, hard-easy

There are two distinct ways in which people tackle life. One path is the hard to easy, and the other is the easy to hard. In a nutshell, the hard-easy path is choosing to do the hard runs up front to then later reap the rewards of the initial hard work. Whereas the easy-hard path will be choosing the easy route first and enduring or suffering the hard part later. People predominately choose one path over another. Depending on the circumstance or the relationship dynamics in a situation, people can select a different path to the one they normally take.

There is no right or wrong in which path you take. Like all choices we make, there are just outcomes. Let's explore each tendency and consider what outcomes might be expected.

The easy-hard path

Choosing the path that is the easiest, cheapest, quickest or most convenient frequently leads to the hard consequences. Often the easy-hard path features lots of chopping and changing because little time is invested in anything. Imagine you are a hungry mouse that discovers a full jar of tasty pellets. Do you take the path of least resistance and begin eating the pellets right away without a further thought? Or, do you take time to plan how to obtain the food without eventually becoming trapped in the jar?

Work

In a work context the easy-hard path is an inclination to bluff and bluster and charm a person's way into a job that is above their skill set, experience and qualifications. Likely the hard part comes about when there is a wide gap between what the job requires and the skills of the person that has feigned their way into the position.

Parenting

The easy-hard parenting path shows little to no boundaries placed around children as they are growing up. Children are given anything they demand just so the parent can have an easy life. An example of this might be a single parent spoiling their child because they are trying to fill the void of an absent parent. Spoiling children may also come about because the parent is compensating for their own strict, controlled childhood. They may be overprotecting their child because their child has disabilities. The child of an easy-hard parenting style becomes permanently dependent on others and has an attitude of entitlement. The consequences of the easy-hard parenting style walks into my clinic on a regular basis. The young adult that sits in front of me displays any mix of the following: feeling lost, lack of motivation, helplessness, anger, recklessness, depression, anxiety, drug addiction, self-harming, being out of control, failing at school.

Health and lifestyle

What does the easy-hard path look like in relationships? Bending the rules, not investing time and energy in communication, failing to learn the needs of your friend or partner and as such only taking from the relationship, taking the easy way out in the form of lying and ghosting.

Eating fast food today leads to ill health later on. Spending money today without consideration of a budget leads to being in debt longer term. Partying today instead of preparing for an exam has its consequences.

Society

Much of our society promotes the easy-hard approach. Politicians, banks, pharmaceutical companies and other organisations all prey on the easy-hard personalities. Banks offer you a credit card meaning you don't have to save or wait a moment longer, but the small print states the interest rate leaps to twenty-four per cent after a honeymoon period! They are counting on you taking out another credit card to pay the interest on the first card. This, of course, is the hard part.

Companies produce cheaper and cheaper goods, then the moment they are out of warranty they break and cannot be repaired, only to be replaced with another cheap version. In this way the purchases become a perpetual expense.

Pharmaceuticals, alcohol and illicit drug sales depend on people demanding an easy fix. When there is emotional pain, or life difficulty, then taking drugs and alcohol gives relief in the short term only for a new issue to show up later – potential addiction – plus the issue that was being avoided in the beginning.

I frequently find the easy-hard approach is used by employers. This is both short-sighted and costly in the long run. For example, salespeople are trained in the basics and then sent out and expected to reach targets. Having no real foundations they fail and eventually leave. In many companies, ninety per cent of all the sales are produced by as little as ten per cent of the personnel.

The hard-easy path

The hard-easy path is about laying great foundations that can be built up to reap the rewards in the long term. This path is about mastering that which gives you meaning. It is about moving towards the challenge, rather than away from it. This path leads to fulfilment and creating a legacy. This path is about conditioning yourself with long-term learning rewards, and not of instant material gratification.

Work

The hard-easy path in work is about investing time learning new skills to land a great job. Having done the work up front and learnt the skills, the tasks of a new job are straightforward and manageable, resulting in relaxation, enjoyment and solid prospects for promotion.

Parenting

The hard-easy path of parenting is about spending time and effort in nurturing the child. These are the parents that do not spoil their kids; they make them wait for things, they encourage learning, they reward on their effort. These parents work on the basis of delayed gratification. The hard-easy parent teaches their children that they are responsible for their actions, they set strong boundaries, they allow them to make decisions within their capability and development level. This type of parenting sets the child up to become an independent and resourceful adult.

Health and lifestyle

I frequently use this hard-easy process in weight management, wealth creation and relationship coaching.

When you're being authentic with your friends and loved ones from the outset of a relationship, it is often challenging, but the long-term benefit is that you don't live in fear of one day being found out. You get to be yourself rather than perpetually living behind a mask.

Hard-easy people spend their time practising the basics over and over until it becomes second nature. When it comes time to perform, it is done with ease. It may be slow to start, but in the long run, it always works out better. The skills that are acquired in the beginning may not always be directly used, but the disciplines developed will be used continually.

Society

These people save their money and then buy the best they can afford.

In organisations, when more resources are spent on training staff up front, the long-term benefits are: retaining staff, greater sales and happier employees.

With making timely hard decisions early, even if you make a mistake you will have the time to test another solution sooner.

> **Time, heat and pressure make diamonds.**

Weighing up the easy-hard and hard-easy roads

- By continuing in easy-hard, it eventually leads to hard-hard.
- By continuing in hard-easy, it eventually leads to easy-easy.

A life of always taking quick-fix options inevitably leads to greater and greater issues. People caught up in an easy way out often end up consuming the resources of those around them. When things start to go from easy to hard for these people, kind-hearted individuals frequently give up their hard-earned money or their precious time to help dig them out of the hole that they created for themselves because they took the easy way first.

Fulfilment is the outcome of the hard-easy trait

The hard-easy trait leads to long-term fulfilment. How do you develop the hard-easy trait? You make a commitment and then consistently persist on that trajectory. In the sunshine, in the rain, when it is easy, when it is hard, and especially when it is inconvenient and when the easy people have all gone home, or to the pub.

When you play the hard-easy game you don't have to be naturally gifted or talented to succeed. By taking the hard-easy road you will simply outlast the crowd.

Does this mean that if you always choose the hard-easy route it will always work out perfectly? No, it definitely will not. However, the easy-hard route usually ends in tears. The hard-easy route may incorporate tears along the way, but the powerful mental and physical foundations lead to longevity and long-lasting fulfilment.

> **I hated every minute of training, but I said, 'Don't quit. Suffer now and live the rest of your life as a champion.'** —Muhammed Ali

Floating above

When you imagine floating above yourself, looking down, you have the ability to see the bigger picture, the context and the reality. You become self-aware. When you are in a hole, you cannot see what is outside that hole, other than you are in a hole and you realise there's another viewpoint from above. The view from above shows you where the hole is, how big it is, where it is located, what other landmarks are close by. There might be others around who can show you insights, and teach you skills to help you get out of the hole.

One of the best such skills is the IOC process, incorporating inquiry, observation and calibration. These three powerful steps are available to apply at any moment to collect perspective and find clarity in any situation. Often a problem, challenge or puzzle can dissolve instantly when you run it through all three steps of the IOC process, in the order described below.

First, prepare for the IOC process by coming to a neutral emotional state. You do this by imagining floating above yourself and looking down. This technique allows you to detach the emotions connected with your problem so you can make decisions with an objective and rational mindset. When you look down on yourself, do you feel any emotional pull or is it quiet and easy and you feel neutral? If there is still emotion present, then float higher until you are feeling neutral.

Each step of the IOC process has a set of questions to answer to help you uncover roadblocks, vital insights and resolutions. For each question, your first response is the one you must take note of because you are looking for the truth stored in your unconscious mind and you are not interested in processing or formulating a conscious answer. If you start digging around for logic, this is when you start to design your response as if manufactured, rather than organic. If you have previously tried and failed to solve your problem with your logical mind, then that is the clue that the answer is not found in that part of your mind. Trust your unconscious mind to tell you the truth.

Inquiry

Inquiry is the initial process to clarify and quantify the puzzle.

Ask yourself these questions:

- Is this really my puzzle to solve or someone else's? It is critical to first work out who owns the problem. If this is not your problem after all, then float back down into your seat, take a deep breath and relax (your work here is done). Respectfully return this puzzle to sender! If you are the owner of it, then proceed to the following questions.

- Why do I need to solve this puzzle?
- What will happen if I don't solve it?
- What will happen if I do solve it?
- Does this puzzle need to be solved, or can I choose another option?
- Is this really a problem or have I made it into a problem because of my intense focus on it?
- Is it the right time to solve it? If not, then relax and come back to it at a future date.
- What's the one question I can ask myself, that if answered would resolve the puzzle right now?

Observation

Observation is using your observation skills to identify why your problem started and has remained in place up until now. In this step, first suspend all judgement and opinion on what answers will come up. Allow them to flow. Notice if you use distractions to avoid hearing them. Distractions such as getting a coffee, ringing a friend, scrolling through your social media, online shopping, getting a snack, going for a cigarette, flicking between your email and the newsfeed, irrelevant self-talk. Humans leak vital information constantly. Observe your answers and your reaction to them; there will be numerous cues for you on how you may have initiated the problem, and how you may be maintaining and driving the problem, without being aware of it.

Ask yourself these questions:
- What is stopping me from resolving this puzzle right now?
- Is this issue held in place by my decisions or beliefs?
- Are any of these decisions faulty or unreasonable?

- Do any of these beliefs come from someone else? If so, I can easily drop the belief and therefore allow the problem to resolve.
- Is someone else telling me it is not right? Or is it truly not sitting right with me?
- Am I ready to take responsibility for my actions?
- Am I ready to be honest with myself and with anyone else this involves?
- Am I ready to offer forgiveness to myself and others where appropriate?
- Am I ready to surrender where it is in my best interest?

Calibration

Calibration is being aware of any emotional distortions and triggers that are affecting the problem-solving process. Calibration is the art of being objective and forming an accurate, unbiased assessment of the situation.

Triggers are formed in your recent or distant past when two things are associated together, so that when one thing occurs, it sets off the other automatically. A classic example of an associative trigger is the dog-conditioning experiment carried out by Nobel Prize winner, Ivan Pavlov, in the 1890s. Every time Pavlov fed his laboratory dogs he would start a metronome (most people recount that he used a bell, but it was a metronome). After repeated pairings of the presentation of food and the metronome, he demonstrated that presenting the ticking sound of the metronome alone was enough for the dogs to know it was dinner time, causing them to salivate in anticipation.

There are thousands of associations you have running as programs unconsciously and outside of your control. Could one of them be salivating to the ticking of a metronome? Jokes aside, without associations we would not be around for long; our survival depends on them. Your job is to calibrate the difference between a survival requirement and an association that is outdated, irrelevant or faulty.

Pivotal Questions:

- Is my problem only a problem because I have a reaction that is associated with something that happened in my past and has nothing to do with the problem at hand?
- What are the triggers in this situation? Can I identify at least two?
- What similar qualities does this problem have to a problem in the past that I'm being triggered by?
- What differences does this problem have to a problem in the past that I'm being triggered by?
- Does thinking about this issue in my past have an emotional loading?
- If the triggers are removed, will the problem dissolve because it's not a real problem?

If you spot it, you got it

A few years ago, during one of my ten-day courses, I was teaching a topic called *Perception and Reality* when one of my beloved students offered up the catchphrase, 'If you spot it, you got it.' The concept I was exploring concerned our tendency of projecting our internal perception onto our external world, while believing the external world has the equal attributes and qualities to that of our internal perception.

To edge closer to reality, the truth of any matter is an ongoing calibration and observation process on your part. At what point does your judgement and internal experience coincide with the purest reality of the external world?

'You're struggling financially,' John says to his friend, Bruce.

'Am I?' says Bruce.

Is John projecting?

Here the important lesson is to understand who owns the belief. Bruce can only know how a situation is for him, and that is his unique perception. John can't be inside Bruce's mind or walk in Bruce's shoes to know his perception. A more respectful and accurate statement by John could be:

'If I had your income and that many children to support, I would be struggling financially.'

Here's another hypothetical situation to demonstrate this concept further. Warren's wife Amanda is the CEO of a big corporation. Amanda abuses Warren and treats him like a second-class citizen. Warren develops anxiety. Warren meets Adam, who also suffers from anxiety. Similarly, Adam's wife is in a high-ranking position within a multi-national corporation. Because of the surface similarities, Warren assumes Adam's anxiety is because of his wife's job and her treatment of him. Adam informs Warren that his anxiety in fact stems from a serious car accident he was involved in last year.

Allison, my partner, told me a story that exemplifies projection perfectly. Allison lived in London for many years before I met her. One afternoon she was queuing at Marylebone Train Station to purchase some snacks. Her queue was long and slow moving. A second queue opened up, and the cashier called 'Next.'

Nobody moved for a number of seconds, so Allison stepped forward to be served. As she began ordering, a huge man of African descent stepped beside her and accused the Indian cashier of being racist for serving Allison before him. Allison, who appears white, tried to explain that she had simply joined the new queue because no one else was paying attention. Uninterested in any explanation she or the cashier could offer, the man began shouting obscenities and calling her racist. He had detected she was Australian by her accent, and stated that she was racist against the Aboriginal people. Little did this abuser know that Allison is Eurasian, and at the time had a boyfriend of part-African descent! To call her racist couldn't have been further from the truth.

After Allison paid for her snacks, the abuser followed her back to a table where four of her friends were seated. There, he began calling her a racist cunt.

'Hey man, there's no need for that,' said one of Allison's friends, who had not been privy to what had transpired in the minutes before.

The man stepped up to her friend and pushed his forehead against his forehead. 'See that CCTV camera? The minute you move out of its line of sight, you're dead.'

Despite the cold threat, Allison would not stand down, because she refused to accept being labelled racist. Allison finally saw what was happening here.

'You know what the real problem is?' she said, staring him straight in the eyes. 'You're the racist one here.'

'You're absolutely right, I hate all white people,' the man admitted.

The greatest gift you can give to yourself and others is to understand that what goes through your mind is all perceptional. What you see in the external world is filtered through your beliefs, values and memories. There is also a perpetual confirmation cycle that persists. We have a strong tendency to see in the external world what you are expecting to see, which then reinforces your belief in that thing. When you reach out to someone to bounce an idea off, what are you really doing? Are you searching for just the right person that you know will tell you what you want to hear, or you truly seeking an objective answer?

When you find yourself projecting, it does not mean that you necessarily display or own that quality. It could be that 'You spot it, you don't want it'. Often, we see a quality in someone else that for ourselves we resist or reject. How many times do you recognise something in your parents, but push against the notion of becoming that yourself? How about the people in your life that you brand a 'bad influence' on you? Let's break that down. When you are being influenced by another in a positive or negative way, it is because some part of you is aligned with the behaviour. That part of you that has an affinity with the 'influenced' behaviour is outside of your conscious awareness. The fact that you can express the behaviour and do not reject it means that you are at cause for it.

You may spot something in someone else that you once had yourself but have since dropped that behaviour. Think of ex-smokers or ex-drinkers.

You may look at someone and notice they are angry. If you are a person with low self-esteem, you may be inclined to project onto that person that the reason they are angry has something to do with you. In reality, it may have nothing whatsoever to do with you. Remember that the emotional response of another person, be it happy, sad or indifferent, is completely on the inside of their nervous system, which has nothing to do with you. Your reaction to that person's emotional response is therefore everything to do with you and nothing to do with them. Again, it is on the inside of your head, in your nervous system.

Learning how to become an observer of yourself is the key to breaking out of this perpetuating cycle of projection and confirmation bias. In doing so it will allow you to live more closely in accordance with reality.

You spot it, you got it exercise

Imagine someone that you are currently having a conflict with is standing in front of you and you are pointing at them in a gesture of blame. Recognise the three fingers pointing back at yourself and determine whether you are projecting by asking yourself:

How do I display that quality I'm blaming another for?
When do I behave like them?
Where did this belief about them come from?
When you point the finger at another in judgement, envy, disapproval, blame or disdain, this is an excellent opening for self-reflection and self-discovery. Those we have relationships with are mirrors into our psyche to varying degrees.

It does not matter if your projection is accurate or not, rather it shows you how you are processing your world and responding to your perceptions of it. In what way are you relating to your external world? Are you in flow with it? Or are you struggling upstream?

You don't go there to find marriage, do you?

Beth and Janet were having their annual get together. They'd been friends for ten years. When they first met, Beth was thirty and single, but always talked of her dream to be married to her Prince Charming, settle down and have kids. When the friends met up each year, the one thing Janet could count on was hearing Beth's woes about not finding her perfect partner. After they had settled into their catch-up, Beth drew a deep breath in preparation to offload her angst. Janet could predict with great accuracy the details of the dating dramas Beth had experienced since they last caught up. Janet would ordinarily comfort and reassure Beth, but this year she'd decided she was going to take a different approach. Beth's broken record problem had become tiresome for Janet, but beyond that, she wanted to help her friend overcome her decade of suffering. Beth began, "I'm forty and desperate to find the love of my life. There are no decent men out there. I've dated five losers this year who have no desire to be in a serious relationship. Why are men so commitment phobic? Why are they only out for fun and flings?" Janet leant forward. "What have you done differently this year to attract the right partner?" she asked. Beth's eyes widened in surprise at Janet's sharp attitude. "What do you mean, different? I checked out a couple of new bars this year and tried the latest dating app, but like I said, all men are the same. I hang out at my local bar every week hoping to meet my Mr Right, but all the nice guys there are either gay or married." Beth threw her hands out in defeat, hoping to extract some sympathy from Janet. Without hesitation, Janet blurted out, "You don't go there to find marriage, do you?"

When you repeat the same actions that lead to the same outcome and you are fully aware of the causality between your actions and the outcome, ask yourself, is this the outcome you desire or is the outcome a problem? If the outcome is a problem, then it's time to revise your actions. If the outcome is what you intended, then your actions and outcomes are aligned perfectly.

If you continue to repeat the same actions and expect a different outcome, discern whether you truly do desire the outcome, or whether you're addicted to having a problem. If you truly desire the outcome, but you acknowledge you are taking actions that perpetuate failure, then discover what the oppositional forces may be and solve those first.

As you progress through this book, an array of possible oppositional forces that are in play will be uncovered. When your awareness expands, your freedom of choice to take a different path opens up. The real power of transformation begins with internal change.

Ignorance is not bliss

As a child, you may have believed that Santa Claus was real. You may have had real conviction in your belief. At some stage, you would have come to the realisation that he was nothing more than a fantasy. Could you ever go back to the same level of conviction? Unlikely. I'm reminded of one of the scenes in *The Matrix*, when Neo is given a choice to take a blue pill and remain in blissful ignorance, or a red pill and learn the painful reality of the fictional computer-generated world he inhabits. This book is like the red or blue pill offering. In the movie, Morpheus says to Neo, 'You take the blue pill – the story ends, you wake up in your bed and believe whatever you want to believe. You take the red pill – you stay in Wonderland and I show you how deep the rabbit hole goes.' After you take the red pill, like Neo, you will not be able to go back. Once you expand your awareness, there is no going back. It's a bit like ignorance: the moment you have wisdom, you can't go back to being ignorant. Are you ready to see?

CHAPTER 3

WHO'S IN THE DRIVER'S SEAT?

Wash your brain

Imagine if you could wash your brain of all the dust and cobwebs and old beliefs and patterns that are weighing you down and holding you back.

We ordinarily understand the word 'brainwash' to refer to being coerced or persuaded, thereby reducing your ability to think critically or independently. You can observe when you or someone else is under a brainwashed state because you or they repeat a statement with no understanding of its meaning. You or they will back up the statement with 'It is because it is' or 'It is because they told me it is'. In a brainwashed stupor you will not be able to bring forth any logic or reasoning to support the belief you are holding. You parrot someone else, but don't understand the concepts behind the information you're regurgitating.

Don Tolman, a health expert and an advocate of self-care and self-education, once conducted a simple human experiment in which he offered a glass of water to a person and asked them to drink it. The person was so sceptical and worried about what could be in the glass that they refused to drink it. He handed them a can of soda and they instantly took the can and drank it without any hesitation. But what did the person think was in the soda? Soda has large quantities of sugar, which is linked to obesity, diabetes and tooth decay. Yet this person would rather drink soda than a glass of water? That is brainwashing at its best.

How often do you trance out in front of the TV, or online streamed content? How often do you scroll aimlessly through your social media feed? All three are packed full of advertising and brainwashing messages. Are you fully aware of what is bypassing your critical thinking and embedding into your unconscious mind? The information on the internet is now heavily censored so you are only seeing what 'they' want you to see. Who are 'they'? They are the powers that fund your platforms and fund much of the mainstream media that ultimately want power over you, your spending habits and voting preferences. You probably believe that propaganda happens in another country less democratic than yours. I'm here to crack through that naivety. The journalists and copywriters behind our mainstream media are told what the narrative should be in line with what whoever owns their butt wants to say. And when I say own, I mean financially and psychologically. Disseminating the truth is a rarity these days unless you are following a reputable independent media source. What you see on commercial TV, or for that matter any mainstream newsfeed, is governed by the agenda of the media mogul or an elite group or politicians sitting behind it. If you are not vigilant, these newsfeeds and so-called current affairs programs are bypassing your critical mind either directly or indirectly and programming you, so your thoughts and actions are just how they designed it. Subliminal messaging through the news and advertising has become an art and a science.

What about brainwashing by your social groups, teachers and your parents? They too have been a significant influence over your ability to express your own freedom of thought and actions.

Perhaps a more accurate and respectful name for this type of brainwashing is social conditioning. Let's focus on your social conditioning and how it directs your day-to-day life and the path your life has been taking. It's time to decondition yourself; drop the programs that are no longer needed or no longer supporting your desired direction. The deconditioning process is about probing your attitudes, actions and beliefs. It is a check-in with your rationale for thinking the way you think or doing the things you do, particularly if they are leading you to a state of conflict. Suspending your autopilot mode and self-reflecting is the best way to identify outdated conditioning. This is about being acutely self-observant of your thoughts and your actions.

A baby only needs to be moments old before it starts to communicate with its parents and be conditioned in return. Most of your core beliefs and behaviours are conditioned in you by the age of seven.

Think of your beliefs and values as conditioned parts of your psyche that serve as your internal compass or your operating system. Your internal compass keeps you alive, running automatically in the background without your conscious awareness. Meanwhile, your smartphone and personal computer require regular updates for their operating systems. Similarly, you and your world change over time, so if you're using an outdated operating system, how slow, clunky, disorganised and inharmonious will your life become?

As soon as you are able to suspend your beliefs and see the unfiltered, unmodified information in front of you, a wider range of options and potential solutions becomes available. This means putting aside the concept of having to be right all the time. Your motivation for knowing the truth is bigger than sustaining an incongruent status. If you keep believing in what you always believed in, then you'll always get what you have always got. Always getting what you always got is a fine position to revel in, but not if you are looking for change.

Thank your parents

Parents are often given a bit of a hard time. In my experience I've found that even the worst parents still do some brilliant things for their children. In fact, the vast majority of what most parents do is fantastic. Do you drive? Do you have a bank account? Do you have the ability to perform basic mathematics? Can you dress yourself and take care of yourself? Even some of the most dysfunctional people in society have much to thank their parents for. Rather than complaining that we don't like what our parents put in our sandwich, we could look at it in more abstract and helpful terms. Think of a baton race in which the baton is handed to the child by the parents in the form of a series of behaviours. The child's job is then to pick up the baton and continue to run. As they run, the child modifies their behaviour to suit the environment before handing the baton on to the next generation. Along the way there will be constructive and deconstructive developments with the baton, but the parents will have done the best job possible with the tools they had at their disposal. If you look at it this way, do you want to complain because you don't like the baton, or say thank you for the baton? Without the baton, we do not exist.

Adapt to survive

Human beings are interesting creatures. If you present a food source, or any form of sustenance, humans will adapt themselves to ensure they get it. In the sixties, the decade of free love, there was a sudden increase in the number of women having children out of wedlock. Various groups formed and decided it would be beneficial to put together a fund for these struggling single parents. What do you think happened? It spawned an entire generation of girls who left school and got pregnant as soon as possible because they knew that having kids would lead to free money from the state. The more kids they had, the more money they would get! Now, there are four generations of these single-parent families. For them, the only career they know of is having babies. Is this right or wrong? It is neither. The fact is that this behaviour has been learned and passed down from generation to generation. Wherever there is a money carrot, we will generate behaviour designed to get that money.

The driver is your unconscious mind

Some of the ancient Eastern philosophies teach a technique called transcendental meditation. The transcendental meditation model implies that we have a conscious mind, an unconscious mind and a higher consciousness. For our purposes, I am specifically interested in the unconscious mind rather than the higher consciousness. Imagine it like a triangle, with the conscious mind at the top being an infinitely tiny proportion of the unconscious mind, which is represented at the bottom. In reality, the conscious mind is probably a drop in the ocean compared to the unconscious mind that is represented by the entire ocean.

In most people's unconscious minds lurk problems of various sizes and levels of complexity. When you first experience something you are not certain how to handle, your nervous system takes over. It puts boundaries around the problem and packages it away in a box in your mind until you have the resources to handle it. These problems can be illustrated by the following scenario I encounter often in my clinic. For the ease of describing this scenario, let's say we have a daughter named Rachel and she has a father called Bill. Bill was a disciplinarian over Rachel when she was a kid, but at the same time demonstrated that he loved her. As a result, Rachel was left with an internal conflict. She was unsure of how to rationalise Bill's two conflicting sides. As a result, Rachel internalised the problem and encapsulated it in her unconscious mind. She drew a boundary around this and placed it in its own neurological box. Later in life, every time she found herself caught between love and discipline in the same way as with Bill, she would put that inside the same box in her unconscious mind. As time passed, the more issues she put inside her Bill box, the bigger the box grew and the thicker the walls became. As a result, more energy was required to keep everything held inside the box. From a neurological perspective, one might refer to this as a 'parts issue'; part of Rachel is conflicted between the two parts, unsure which one to guide her. The more intense the conflict, the more energy required to keep it all contained in the box.

During meditation you enter into your unconscious mind. If you happen to hit a box, it opens and releases the contents. You would experience that as a release of energy; some people may cry; others may laugh and some may yawn. All of these responses are an expression of energy. One of the main differences between meditation and what you are learning here is that meditation is very good at going after the little boxes. However, if there is a huge box presented, that is likely to represent a high degree of pain and discomfort. So, whilst you are dropping deeper into your unconscious mind during meditation, you are likely to do everything you can to avoid the big boxes.

One of the issues with meditation is that it may take you years to open the big boxes. Why? Because it represents pain, and every time you personally attempt to address it or touch it, you experience that pain in all its menacing glory. Your own clever survival mechanisms may prevent you from ever dealing with it.

The way you deal with your emotions and history is that they are processed at an unconscious level. Sometimes this takes us in a direction we choose and sometimes in a direction we have not consciously chosen. Your conscious mind may want to go in a certain direction, but if your unconscious mind is programmed to do the opposite, it will do just that. A sense of calm will be reached only when your conscious mind and your unconscious mind are in sync with each other; they align with each other. You see, your unconscious mind is on autopilot. When you are consciously aware that your unconscious mind is pulling you in the 'wrong' direction, you can pull it back into line with your conscious mind. However, the moment you're not holding on to that conscious thought, the compass will realign to what it was programmed to do.

If you have resisted making changes up to now, I'm guessing you've been feeling a whole lot of pain in your life. It really will be more painful if you just keep doing the same thing over and over again. Make the changes you need. How easy is it to make a change? Think of a time when you forgot where you'd left your keys. From that moment on, you decided to create your own system to help you remember to always put the keys in your pocket. You effectively created your own change program. Change is that easy! Seeing another way and making different choices results in change.

Emotional driving

Do your emotions send you out of control at times, as if they are driving your car with you trapped helpless and blindfolded in the passenger seat? Do you sometimes feel you're in an emotional haze? Do you often make poor decisions because of emotional triggers or baggage? Or do you feel empty and numb? How would you feel if you could gain greater emotional flow?

Have you ever had a memory so powerful that you only had to think about it and you would be back there, experiencing those emotions like it was happening right now and leading you to feel angry, guilty, ashamed, frustrated, anxious, fearful or sad? On the flip side, do you recognise when emotions such as exhilaration, joy and happiness lift you up and take you off in a direction? Just remembering an event could give you a strange sensation in your stomach, your heart or your throat. As we discussed in Chapter 1, memory is a powerful thing. Emotions connect you to historical events that trick you into feeling the event is happening right now. It's where your brain and body become one. There is a chemical exchange that occurs in the body that drives us into action. Every time you have an emotion, your physiology changes.

What do you think would happen if you were fearful all the time, day after day, month after month, year after year? Chronic stress and anxiety have been linked to obesity, cardiovascular disease and cancer.

The way you handle emotions is put in place when you are very young, usually before the age of seven. As you live your life and experience the highs and lows of being human, we collect a bagful of old emotions that are attached to memories. What would happen if you could drop the old negative emotions attached to a memory of a historical event but retain the value in the wisdom of the experience?

I'm a big fan of emotions that flow, as opposed to being controlled. In traditional Chinese medicine, physical and mental wellbeing is all about energy flowing evenly and smoothly.

Addressing the triggers of intense or suppressed emotions is the key to good flow. When emotions become trapped, so does energy. Over time, trapped energy causes a myriad of musculoskeletal complaints, organ sluggishness and systemic malfunction. Your body will feel contracted and tight. Your breath will be affected. It may be that you begin to hold your breath, or your breath may be shallow, fast or irregular – all unhealthy breath patterns.

The beauty of the mind and body being one system is that conditioning one area has a consequent effect on the other. Condition your emotions to flow and your body will become healthy, supple and vibrant. Conditioning and moving your body will help to release trapped emotions and also encourage energy flow. Which one to tackle first? Conditioning both in parallel will give you a greater result than the sum of the individual parts. In this way the mind and body are spiralling upwards in unison.

Cognitive Behavioural Therapy (CBT) is one of the first tools many professionals in the field of psychology and behavioural therapy reach for. Unfortunately, this tool requires the client to use their rational thought processes for it to work. However, a rational thought process is absent the moment adrenaline is released into a person's system; logic and rationality go out the window. When a person enters a fear, anxiety or stress state by means of an unconscious reaction to a trigger event or thought, all cognitive sense evaporates.

Changing your perceptions is the key. Being present in the moment is essential to resolving emotions such as fear. Fear can occur to anyone, at any moment in time. So, what is fear? It is your mind doing its job. An external piece of stimulus that is linked to an unconscious perception of imminent danger leads to a fear state. In plain terms, tigers eat people, so they're dangerous. If you come face to face with a tiger, run away now, no thinking required. The only problem is if we are in a situation where we can't run. This is made even worse by the people around us all looking at the tiger that we absolutely know will kill us, saying: 'What tiger? There is no tiger. This is not a tiger'.

The tiger of fear is often a physical sensation that is accompanied by an internal image. The solution is changing the structure of the feelings and sensations by removing or modifying the triggers. This is done by changing the building blocks of one's reality. As a result, the link between the external stimulus and the internal association is permanently broken. It is magical to witness. Often you will deny the tiger ever existed. Thankfully most of us never encounter a real tiger. Our tigers are simply perceptional predators. Just before the fear starts to rise, notice what you are thinking and what you are telling yourself about a past or future scenario. Often fear follows your thoughts that begin with 'What if…', imagining a horrible prospect of something in the future. Reality can only be experienced in the moment.

Unlike real predators, perceptional predators can be slayed from the comfort of your armchair. How do you know what your perceptional monsters are? This is what Part II of this book is all about. You'll discover how you uniquely process reality, your limiting beliefs, how your childhood conditioning plays a part, how you filter away vital information, how to identify your neurotic behaviours and thoughts, and learn to understand your triggers.

If you aren't in charge of your reactions and your nervous system, then who is? You are in charge of your perceptions and responses. Again, who is to say that walking around happy is better than walking around pissed off? Your emotional state is the radio station that you listen to in your car on your journey to your destination. You can tune in to whichever radio station you wish. As far as the river of life is concerned, it doesn't matter if you're listening to a death march or a top forty song, the journey will continue on. My question to you is what would you like to be listening to?

Freedom monsters

Understanding the concepts of slavery and freedom are key facets to being a well-balanced human. I learnt long ago that there was no such thing as a well-adjusted slave. This is an interesting sentence, but what does it mean? Firstly, the idea of freedom in your external world is a complete fantasy. It's just a fairy-tale. Being alive means that hunger binds us, gravity and time dictate to us, and only in death are we free of these constraints.

The number of rules and regulations, laws and taxes are incredible. Most of these laws are enacted not by common law but admiralty law. Another way of describing admiralty law is to think of it as the law of commerce. Even the act of obtaining a birth certificate creates the legal fiction that is your personal bill of loading. Simply put, you are the property of the state. When you register a car, you are handing the control of it to the state. The word registration comes from Regi (King), Regina (Queen). Even when you buy land it is never really yours. What you are buying can be taken away very easily. Do you own the water on your land? No. Do you own the minerals below your feet? No. At this point you might be thinking, Robb, are you an anarchist? No. This is just the way it is; it has been this way for thousands of years.

We are more surveilled and controlled now than ever before. In the last one hundred years, it is estimated that one billion people have been killed or died fighting for the concept of freedom. Fighting for freedom is the one sure way of ensuring slavery. This is achieved by creating a fictitious monster that you must fight against, or it will be the death of you and all that you love. As you fight against this fictitious monster, you hand resources over to the creator of the monster. This process of creating monsters to manipulate others is not just about governments; it is also about our social groups too. Families do it to each other, lovers do it, churches do it, and why? Because people fall for the illusion of monsters. Guys, this is a stupidity test or a stupidity tax which we are all failing or passing depending on your point of view.

Does freedom exist? Yes, it does. Freedom occurs the moment you start seeing the monsters for what they are: illusions. Like the shadows of fingers with light behind them dancing on a cave wall, your fears are just created within you. I was fortunate to learn this lesson long ago in martial arts. The fear of getting hit is far more damaging than the hit itself. The fear of being hit is the very thing that guarantees you will be hit. Does not having a fear of the illusion mean that you will never be hit? No. Danger is real and exists in the physical world. Fear exists only in the story we tell ourselves. The real skill is to recognise the difference between the story and the reality. Once you learn this skill, you will see danger coming from miles away and have the best possible chance of stepping out of its way.

The ideal is for you to recognise your personal monsters for what they are: illusions created by others and believed by you to trick you into giving up your resources. The most valuable resource of all is your time. By the way, monsters come in all shapes and sizes and are enmeshed with money, love, relationships, sex, health, education and so on. As you deal with each monster, your freedom grows. No sooner have you gained your freedom from one monster then the next will appear. Remember, we all create monsters or illusions to make sense of this world. The ability to remove the monsters is the process of becoming disillusioned (the removal of illusion). Some would say we just replace one illusion with a more inclusive or friendlier one.

> **Have fun making friends with your monsters; it is the path to true freedom.**

Depression and decompression

Without doubt, over the last thirty years the one condition that sits in my clinic chair more than any other is depression. Often individuals walk into my clinic as they are seeking rapid results. They have been told by other professionals they have depression and it's going to take a long time to overcome it and/or they need to take medication. Indeed, many individuals are unaware of the fact that depression can be solved and need not be endured for years to come.

So, what is depression? It is a set of mental and physical symptoms that we all suffer from time to time as a natural part of being alive. The real issue is when it becomes our daily method of operation and steals our life force.

Symptoms may include:

- No interest in doing things
- Emotional feelings of unhappiness or hopelessness
- Physical feelings of being rundown, having little to no energy
- Sleep issues: too much, too little, difficulty falling asleep, difficulty rising
- No appetite or overeating
- Constant rumination of 'I am a failure', 'not good enough', 'I am letting my family or team down'
- Issues with concentration

- Body language may consist of a bowed head and a sad expression
- Moving slowly, speaking slowly, everything is accompanied with a deep sigh (opposite symptoms can also be experienced, for example, rapid movement and agitation)
- Suicidal thoughts on an ongoing basis

Depression can be solved rapidly and painlessly if you come at it from the right direction.

> A man stands by the side of his car with the bonnet up and smoke and steam coming from the engine. The mechanic standing beside him states that it has blown up because there is no oil in the engine. 'Didn't you see the red light on the dashboard?' The man replies, 'Yeah, I saw the light, so I used my chewing gum to cover it up.'

Unfortunately, many people use this Band-Aid approach to the whole subject of depression. They use drugs and other distractions so that they don't have to look at the red light on the dashboard, indicating the symptoms leading to depression. The consequences are that the distractions increase until something breaks: health, wealth or happiness.

The areas of your life feeding the depression are the red lights on the dashboard. To solve them, you need to deal with your stuff. This is about addressing the things that are perpetuating the state. What are these things? They are the circumstances you may be choosing to be in, and your response to them, your unhelpful thoughts, damaging behaviours and decisions, inflexible beliefs, and lifelong outdated conditioning. Unresolved fear leads to anger, unresolved anger leads to sadness and unresolved long-term sadness leads to depression. With this in mind step one is to resolve any disproportionate fear. Fear is a state of compression, so the way out is to decompress. The pathway to resolving fear is about expanding awareness, expanding your mind and your body to new opportunities and possibilities. It is about opening up to new ways of thinking. Expanding your body is exercising and moving it and freeing it up so the energy can flow and give you increased vitality. With vitality, you have the endurance to propel yourself into exploring new terrain for dissolving any dysfunctional, irrational fear.

In Part III: Transformation, you will discover two self-help methods directed at resolving fear and other stuck emotions. These self-help methods are: Presence of body beats presence of mind, and Fast freedom forward.

Fear is perceptional. You may have noticed that we have been loosening faulty perceptions all the way through the book and this theme is woven throughout the rest of the book. If you truly understand your reality is perceptional, then you can put this book down right now and skip off into the sunset.

Oh, good grief

'Oh, good grief' was a famous catchphrase of the cartoon character, Charlie Brown. It was usually the result of a situation that didn't work out the way it was supposed to. Life is like that. While things usually work out in the end, 'working out' may not entail exactly what you expected. In fact, things working out might just be your worst nightmare. In the grand scheme of things, we are born, we live and then we die. If we accept these three basic facts as being the only sureties in life, it becomes harder to become disappointed.

Disappointment occurs at the point where we have an expectation of a thing happening, and then it doesn't happen. Believing in the one true love of your life would be an expectation. Discovering that your one true love has been sleeping with the entire volleyball team, stealing from your bank account or hates your guts would be a disappointment. When the physical reality doesn't match the internal images that we have previously created, then we experience this as frustration.

Grief, on the other hand, is the point in which we are reaching for a thing or a person that is no longer there. Often it is associated with the death of someone you loved, though it could be virtually anything that you were once physically associated with, that has now gone for whatever reason.

Grief is also the natural process of rebuilding neural connections. Another way of thinking about it is as the process of unlearning. Grief can be experienced by anyone at any time. It may be the unlearning of a mother after her children have left the nest. It may be the unlearning of a retired worker who is no longer in that position, with the associated feeling of being valued. One visitor to my clinic chair was a middle-aged woman who had previously used her sexuality and attraction qualities to open doors. She entered a stage of intense grief when men and women no longer turned to look at her.

When unlearning, rebuilding and making new memories, time is required. Experiencing new people and situations will rebuild new neural networks. In your own time, you will make new memories where you will reach less and less for the historical things and people in your life. It begins with your decision to begin rebuilding. Grief is a normal and natural process of being human and it can even be triggered by leaving your warm bed on a winter's morning.

The river of life

> One famous tale from Eastern philosophy tells of Confucius walking with a number of followers to a river that had a reputation as a suicide destination. Unhappy people would end their lives there by jumping into the rapidly moving currents. As they were walking, the followers saw an elderly man jump into the river. Everybody was upset by what they saw, so Confucius instructed them to run down and drag the body from the river. However, as they were running, they encountered the old man walking back from the river completely unharmed. 'You're lucky to survive!' they exclaimed. The old man replied, 'No, I have been doing this for years.' Curious, the students asked how this was possible as the river was so powerful and dangerous. The old man's response was simple. 'The river is infinitely more powerful than I will ever be, so when it pushes me down, I take a breath; when it pushes me to the left, I move to the left; when it pushes me to the right, I go to the right. When it pushes me close to the shore, I reach up, grab a branch and swing to shore.'

How many of us flounder and fight against the river of life? Do you often become emotionally reactive and unable to think straight? Or do you suppress your emotions? Trying to fight the river will ensure you will drown, unless you are able to harness the energy of your emotions to direct your actions.

In the next section, Jane Nash, who co-trained my students in my psychotherapy course, will lead you through a beautiful resource-building piece around options. Jane is an author of several books, a psychotherapist and a master trainer of over fifteen years.

Boxes of apples
By Jane Nash

I have spent some time learning some new skills. Oh, I know I'm always learning and extending my skills, but here is an area I'd love to share. I've learned how options are like apples and everyone deserves to have a box of them delivered from time to time. Well, seriously, I have learned to ask better questions. Better questions of others and of myself. 'Where do you want to go?', 'What do you want to achieve?' and 'Who do you want to become?'

My grandmother can't go very far, physically relying on a walker/trolley for mobility and under lockdown restrictions in England. The question 'Where do you want to go?' seems trite and disrespectful. My grandmother is now nearly blind. I ask her this question, and I know she is resigning herself to the status quo but on her face, I see the spark of memory listing her previous adventures. Then, there is something more. In the same way my voice goes with my clients when they are in hypnosis, so does my grandmother with me when I reach out into the world. She goes with me. I know this because at 7.15 every morning I take her there via FaceTime through meetings, social gatherings and interesting stories I've written, read or experienced. 'Where do you want to go?' The answer is not just through her memories now that she is confined by her lack of sight, limited mobility and government restrictions, but to go with me and live life through me. I am happy to carry her with me.

I asked a client, 'What do you want?' She told me she wanted to not drink a second glass of wine, or a third glass or a fourth. So, I asked her again, 'What do you want?' To want the absence of something is too problematic for many to achieve. Goals need well-formed steps and conditions. The absence of something lacks the posts through which to score. She wanted to be able to have a single glass of wine without ... and there again she threw herself into another negative space. But nature abhors a vacuum. To create a negative space is opening an invitation for its immediate occupancy. We exchanged challenges, (one of the more fun types of conversation) and it became clear quite quickly that her problem with how she was, when drinking too much, was in fact the same state as when she was sober – she was trying to create options for herself. Alcohol had just provided her with different options. She was still in the process of creating freedom for herself to choose in life. What did she want? Together, we coded the desired state of mind and it became apparent that apples had become a symbol for options, and she wanted a box of them, not just for herself, but also for the person who had been denying her options throughout her life. She wasn't angry. She was compassionate and ultimately neutral about her emotional need to drink more than one glass of wine. All I did was ask and re-ask a very good question.

My niece is twelve, and being an absent aunty, I live largely in FaceTime. I see her grow in leaps and bounds. She becomes more like Rapunzel with each living second, except perhaps more of a cheerleading Rapunzel. She is as close to my mother as I am to my grandmother, and as I watch her grow, I am tempted to ask her what may seem like a serious question for a twelve-year-old: 'Who do you want to become?' Of course, her experience of the world is exceptionally limited, even with access to online communities. I buy a teen empowerment book for her Christmas present, hoping to inspire her to take note of Helen Sharman, the first British astronaut, the very great, and sadly late, Ruth Bader Ginsberg of the US Supreme Court. I want her to be inspired by Graça Machel, politician and humanitarian, to name but a few. I want her to, I want her to, I want her to ... It is then that I realise, 'Who do you want to become?' is not a question for her but for me. Even at fifty-one. I still 'want to become' something like those women. I too want to walk on broken glass and feel the wind in my long hair. Recently, finally, my actions have begun to reflect this.

I have learnt to ask better questions and in that learning, I have discovered I am as unsophisticated as a child, as wise as an ancient and as unformed as that block. I am still uncarved. I am beginning to like the rugged hewn landscape of my current investigations. I can't travel abroad to search out new and interesting cultures, I can't fly to visit my family, but I can ask of myself, 'How can I have more fun doing this?' And I ask it when I am working or meeting deadlines or focusing on providing my husband and me with more apples. It's surprising how many apples there are in life if you look for them.

I've another good question for you: 'What do I have to be grateful for?' There is a science behind gratitude. Gratitude activates the central and dorsal medial pre-frontal cortex. It triggers the production of dopamine, serotonin and oxytocin through the stimulation of feelings of reward without stress, morality, interpersonal bonding and positive social interactions. It reduces the need for us to compare ourselves with each other. I know that as a therapist I have asked of my clients, 'Do you practice gratitude?' but since Covid times, the question is now precise and unabashed in its asking. 'What do you have to be grateful for?'

Through these Covid times I have also been participating in a series of conversations with Rob McNeilly, an ex-pupil of the late Milton H. Erickson, (the incredible psychiatrist and clinical hypnotherapist) and others also interested in Erickson's work. Here I learned a few more excellent questions, and these have become the base of my problem solving. I thought I'd share them with you to see if they spark anything in you, because they are after all, excellent.

'What do you like?' That's a bit like 'What do you want?' but it's more immediate and it anchors you into an experience. 'What is it about it that you like?' Good questions elicit specific answers. Understanding the key drivers or motivations about an experience is like having the answers to a quiz. 'What is the problem?' Again, a nice, specific question, but get this next one: 'How is the problem the same as the thing you like?' Head turning, neck smacking and annoying – because it's true. Think hard enough and you'll be able to see the connection. There is always a connection. And now I've written them down I am inclined to say, ask those questions in any order you like, because they will be your questions and not mine. But they will, most definitely, bring about a transderivational search (both sides of the brain working), which will put you into a most resourceful state of mind (trance) for problem solving.

So here I am. Fingers hovering over the keyboard, boxes of apples next to the fridge and questions to stimulate the unconscious mind.

Possibility vs necessity

We live in a world of infinite possibility. However, so many of us operate as people of necessity. The famous Double Slit experiment presented in the 2006 docudrama *What the Bleep Do We Know!? Down the Rabbit Hole* demonstrates that tiny particles of matter such as photons, when fired at a barrier containing two slits, will always produce completely different wave patterns on the other side of the barrier. Why is this? When the experiment is being observed by someone, the wave pattern changes. In fact, the scientists showed that the observed particles ended up being in two places simultaneously. Imagine that: the mere fact that someone is observing the experiment changes the very nature of matter and energy.

What I take from this experiment is that existence is based on energy and infinite possibility. The moment you look at something, the moment you observe something, it changes. We have waves of infinite possibility all around us and this is where imagination and creativity emerge from.

This is one of the lessons we can take from quantum physics. When you observe an object, it can change into a monster, or a vision of beauty, depending on your state of mind or the angle of observation. Also, the qualities change depending on who is observing it. Your perceptional position determines your moment-to-moment reality.

We are trained to live in a way that dictates necessity. Even the word 'necessity' breeds anxiety. You might say 'I need to exercise every day.' The moment you change the word 'need', which is a necessity-loaded word, to a possibility word, the anxiety about what you must do is removed. A possibility statement would be 'I look forward to exercising every day' or, 'I choose to enjoy exercising every day.'

Stress is often founded in necessities. I must get that job, I must be a perfect son, I must get those grades, I must have that car, I must be successful, I must, I must, I must ... What would happen if instead of becoming stressed with all of the things you must do, you just chilled out and changed your attitude to *possibility* instead of necessity? Do you think you would feel more relaxed?

I was just today listening to a fascinating YouTube presentation by Dr Andrew Huberman, an American Neuroscientist. His research shows that individuals are unconsciously wired to maintain their beliefs because they receive a dopamine surge when they are able to reassert a belief with selected evidence in their environment. This propensity to receive the dopamine hit rather than seek truth also leads us away from possibility at an unconscious level. Your practise is to observe your own beliefs and whether you are overlooking reasonable and sensible facts just so you can receive the righteousness dopamine fix.

I'm wondering if you've now discovered some specifics of what brought you here. Having now completed Part I, how has learning your blind spots and expanding your perceptions changed your reality?

> **We've added years to life, not life to years. —Dr Bob Moorehead**

The purpose of this book is to guide
you in adding life to years.

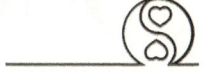

PART II

Building Solid Foundations

PART II GUIDES YOU through creating the foundations of a good life. You will discover the real you beneath the conditioning and beliefs of who you think you are or who you've been told you are. You'll gain insights into why you do the stuff you do and why you feel the way you do. Your understanding of what is perception and what is reality will shift your mindset of problem into solution rapidly. I'll guide you in a number of techniques that you can plug in for instant results. On completing this part, you'll have tidied up your stuff and made room for transformation.

CHAPTER 4

THE CONNECTED WHOLE

Mind your body

> Man [...] sacrifices his health in order to make money. Then he sacrifices money to recuperate his health. [...] he lives as if he is never going to die, and then dies having never really lived. —Dalai Lama

Being healthy is making health the first point of your focus. Begin with a foundation of health and all the layers of your life will flow more easily.

When you're searching for a romantic mate, think how much more attractive is a healthy person. You're more inclined to look twice if they still have all their teeth and boast good skin, good muscle tone and shining eyes.

When you're studying and your head is clear, how inspired do you feel?

When you're alert at work and you see all your colleagues around you wired with caffeine or snoozing without, how empowered do you feel?

When your kids are running around the backyard and you can keep up with them, despite being fifty years old, how amazing is that?

When you travel the world and climb mountains in your seventies, how inspirational are you to others?

Energy flow

Avoiding an area of emotional pain is like avoiding a tear in your skin. Tending to the wound, taking care of it and treating it appropriately will lead to rapid healing. In contrast, picking at it, damaging the same area over and over will create a deeper wound and a lasting scar. If you avoid looking after it, the wound can become infected and affect other areas of your body. If you decide to partition the wound off with a tight tourniquet, directing energy away from it, healing stops. The area eventually becomes numb and inactive, and you lose a part of you as it becomes disconnected from your awareness. Continue doing this to other parts of your body and you become less and less whole. You become fragmented. Imagine if you no longer had the use of your right leg and your right arm because they had been disconnected from the rest of your body. You could still hop around with a crutch, but your movement and ability to fully experience life would be limited.

In exactly the same way your body becomes fragmented, your mind can become fragmented when you avoid addressing the source of emotional pain. In this fragmented state, what are some of the outcomes that could follow? Anxiety, depression and psychoses are some of the more serious states. At the very least, your level of fulfilment would be compromised.

Perceptional predators

Fear is produced in our society primarily because of what we refer to as perceptional predators. These are not literal predators. How many times have you been chased by a tiger in the last three weeks? Perceptional predators are things that cause fear and stress with the same type of chemical reactions that would occur when actually being chased by a tiger. Your body does not know the chemical difference between a real threat and a perceptional threat, because as far as your body is concerned, it's all about survival.

Real predators are rare and if you do meet one, there will be a short-lived spurt of fear to force you to act now to ensure you escape the attack (fight or flight response). Meanwhile, perceptional predators can last for prolonged periods of time; they can become unrelenting because they're driven by the mind. It is highly likely these perceptional predators are affecting you on a daily basis, meaning that your adrenal glands are constantly being fired up. This is doing real harm to you, your quality of life, your life expectancy.

Chronic fear can lead to burnout, which in medical terms is adrenal exhaustion. There are a multitude of repercussions that go with this, including digestive problems, lower back pain, toxic overload, fuzzy head, heart problems and memory lapses. The adrenal glands are meant to react to situations in short bursts to provide you with much-needed energy in an urgent situation. However, if you are living in a constant state of fear, the glands will reach a point of exhaustion and you will lose the ability to function. In the context of Traditional Chinese Medicine, how much adrenal energy you have left in reserve is directly related to how long you have left to live.

Your body has super intelligence and continually adapts to keep you alive. During a state of fear, your blood is redirected away from the intestines and into the limbs, and blood flow to the frontal lobe of your brain is reduced; the advanced part of our brain that performs reasoning. In a state of fear, your ability to digest food is compromised and instead of digesting food in an efficient, healthy way, the body has to make a decision about how to deal with it. By this point there is not enough energy to digest it efficiently, as the whole system becomes compromised. By not digesting food effectively, your cells become depleted of the essential nutrition and minerals that it needs for your body to function optimally. When you are experiencing chronic fear, the propensity of storing fat increases as it requires the least energy. Furthermore, the past forty years have seen an explosion in environmental toxins in our water, soil, air and food. Our bodies are miraculous at excreting and handling toxins, but not when we are chronically stressed! This means that when you are chronically stressed, you are also likely to be toxically loaded, which causes a myriad of other health problems.

Mind your gut

Do you suffer from a 'stress-belly' (excess fat around your midline)? Do you have bowel issues, skin rashes, immunity problems such as allergies, brain fog, memory challenges, joint pain and stiffness, ongoing general illnesses, anxiety, depression, other mental health issues? Do you frequently get sick when you go on holiday? If you answer yes to any of these, then you are likely to be chronically stressed. The link between the mind and many of these health issues is due to the load on the system that has weakened your adrenals and compromised your gut (gastrointestinal system). The brain and gut are both physically and biochemically connected. I see them as one and the same system. Your gut is the master of immune health. Chronic long-term stress impacts your digestion and suppresses your immune system, which opens the door to opportunistic parasites and bacteria. It's a double-edged sword, because with a suppressed immune system, your ability to protect yourself against these invaders and environmental toxins has been compromised. When the body cannot process or eliminate toxins, they are stored in body fat and in lymphatic tissue to protect you. When your body becomes oversaturated with toxins, your body is open to disease. When you find it hard to lose excess weight, it may have more to do with your level of fear and less about what you're eating or how much you're exercising. In fact, strict dieting and extreme exercise regimes are also forms of stress. So, pay close attention to what is healthy and supportive and what is obsession, addiction or distraction.

Not only does your nervous system impact your gut, but the opposing affectation is so crucial to understand as well; your gut health affects your mental health. The strong link between poor gut health and mental health issues such as autism, attention deficit hyperactivity disorder, epilepsy, anxiety, depression and schizophrenia have been widely studied and documented. Serotonin is our natural 'happy drug' and a whopping ninety per cent of serotonin is produced in your gut. Do you sense when you are having a gut feeling about something? Your brain and your gut are in deep conversation. Minding your mind is about caring for your body.

The mind and body are one

The mind and the body are one. So much so, that you can successfully train for a physical activity by practising it in your mind. A university research group tested this using basketball training with three groups of basketball players. The first group simply trained and played basketball as usual. The second group doubled the amount of training. The third group trained as usual and spent time sitting on the benches, practising shooting hoops in their imagination. When it came time to test them physically, the third group scored the highest. The third group were getting it right every time in their minds, so when they came to shoot in reality, their muscle movements corresponded with what they had practised in their imagination, allowing them to replicate the same results. As you think, so your body will respond. This methodology is now used worldwide by elite athletes, with applications in education, health and business.

CHAPTER 5

YOU'RE ON THE PATH TO FULFILMENT

Living in the Tao

Going with the flow of life can be easier said than done, as is the advice from Eckhart Tolle to 'live in the now'.

The stress and strain of life arise from internal conflicts. These conflicts come in the form of having an image, concept or expectation on the inside of your head that is different from the stuff that is happening on the outside 'reality'. Winding yourself into a stressful state often arises out of your thoughts alone. I'm going to share with you two solutions for stress.

The first solution is the most practical and tangible method, which involves your observation and calibration skills. You will identify where your internal world is not aligned with what is happening in your external world.

Stress means being in a particular situation, circumstance or position in the here and now, while perpetuating an attitude and a desire of wanting it to be different. Stress can mean imagining something that is going to happen in the future that you can't control, with potential negative consequences. It can be that deadline that you imagine you're going to miss, or the trouble you think you're going to get in for not paying your parking fine, or the imagined future breakdown of your currently wonderful relationship. Being pressured to do something outside of your morals, values and ethics can also place considerable stress on you.

The solution is to bring your mind back to what you are experiencing in the now: what is real, right now. This doesn't mean you can't think of the past or the future, but experiencing the present can be instantaneously calming since the present moment is the only time you can change your response to an external pressure happening in this moment. Your thoughts drifting off into the past or future can take you into a place of powerlessness and being overwhelmed. This first solution is to simply observe how your thoughts alone bring about the stress, and not any actual eventuation of an imagined negative or painful event. Changing your thoughts is an underestimated power that you have in your hands right now.

Animals don't stress about tomorrow; they only think about the now. Experiencing starvation, being deprived of water or being exposed to harsh environmental, life-threatening conditions are situations to be truly stressed about, since they are real threats to life. If you are reading this book, it is unlikely you are in a state of starvation. Our developed world stresses come from living in the zone of wants rather than needs. Stress is overextending yourself beyond your means and energy. It's the credit card that's overflowing with debt, it's the mortgage you can't meet, it's the cost of running that luxury car. It's doing a job that you don't have the skills for but have bluffed your way into. It's the taking on responsibility that you have no control over. It's juggling too many commitments. It's spreading yourself too thin in attempting to help too many people. Dissolving stress is about making choices that align with your core values and following your chosen path to perpetuating personal fulfilment.

The questions below will help you to pinpoint the origin of any stress. Once you've identified the origin, then you can address it.

- Do you have unreasonable expectations on yourself, or from others?
- Do you have healthy boundaries in your relationships?
- Are you being triggered by something from your history?
- Is it your problem, anyway? Who owns this problem?
- Are you taking responsibility for something that is outside of your control or influence?
- Are your sentences starting with the words 'I should' or 'I must'?
- Are your thoughts and actions a conditioned response from your history?
- Are you under the illusion that stress helps you work faster and harder?
- Are you searching for love, acceptance, validation and recognition outside of yourself?
- Do you avoid expressing yourself because you worry it will create conflict or fighting?
- Are you addicted to being in a state of stress?

How did you go with your answers? Revealing? Did you pinpoint key areas where the stress is originating from, and in so doing can address those areas with a sense of purpose and clarity?

Know that you always are doing your best, and that you are enough right here and now. Building your sense of self-worth and valuing yourself as the most important person in the world is paramount to achieving relaxation and going with the flow of life.

The second solution to stress is living in accordance with a Taoist life. I call it 'Living in the Tao'. Tao is pronounced 'dow' like the word 'dowel' without the 'el'. The 'T' in Chinese is pronounced 'D'. I studied Taoism during my Traditional Chinese Medicine diploma. Although I never announced this to my students in my classes nor to my clients, I live my life by closely following Taoist principles. Taoism is not a religion; it is a Chinese philosophy developed by Lao Tzu (c.500 BCE). Taoism emphasises going with the flow of nature. The way of the Tao often flies in the face of the ideology of the modern, fast-paced, competitive capitalist society. The way of the Tao is the more you live in flow, the more you experience a deeper richness to life.

The *Tao-Te-Ching* is a book of poetry which describes the Taoist principles. Its title can be translated to: *Book of the Way and Of Virtue*. I highly recommend reading this book. It changed my life in a powerfully positive way. Here is a sample of timeless philosophical gestures from the *Tao-Te-Ching*.

- How do I know the way of all things at the Beginning? By what is within me.
- To return to the root is to find peace. To find peace is to fulfil one's destiny.
- Only simple and quiet words will ripen of themselves. For a whirlwind does not last a whole morning. Nor does a sudden shower last a whole day.
- Heaviness is the root of lightness.
- Serenity is the master of restlessness.
- He who knows men is clever. He who knows himself has insight. He who conquers men has force. He who conquers himself is truly strong.
- There is no calamity like not knowing what is enough.

- There is no evil like covetousness.
- Only he who knows what is enough will always have enough.
- Use the lights but return to your insight.
- Big things of the world can only be achieved by attending to their small beginnings.
- Tackle things before they have appeared.
- Cultivate peace and order before confusion and disorder have set in.

Dropping righteousness and opening up to learning new perspectives will lead you to new answers. Instead of clinging to the beliefs of your past conditioning, you can open yourself to a flexibility to choose what is in sync with what is happening in the present. It can feel uncomfortable and uncertain as it is new territory, and that is part of the new game you'll be playing where you'll be rewarded with the prize of fulfilment.

Happiness, fulfilment and love

Happiness, fulfilment and love are foundations of living a good life.

I like to teach the concept of happiness as being one pillar. True, unwavering permanent happiness is a mindset, a feeling in your body that gives you a sensation of wholeness. True happiness is purely an internal knowing that you are divine and your state of being is not conditional on the happenings on the outside of you. It is your birthright to be happy, no matter what. The happiness state is an advanced prospect, and eludes so many of us. We may grab glimpses of what we think is happiness but because it is fleeting, you will know it is not true happiness. When we talk of the happiness in our lives, what I believe we are really referring to is fulfilment, and this state does not add or subtract from happiness: they are mutually exclusive states.

Let's look at the various ways to build fulfilment in your life. The easiest way to categorise fulfilment is by time. Short, medium and long term, one could say the concept of fulfilment has a similarity to a healthy diet. There are foods you like but aren't that good for you. There are foods that are not that exciting but in the long run are significantly better for you. This doesn't remove the fact that we are all addicts. We are all looking for our daily emotional fix; the question is, what is your drug of choice? Just like some people choose juice over spirits or water over wine, so too is your choice of fulfilment type. No right or wrong, just a decision, benefits and outcomes.

Let's start with short-term fulfilment. These are items or activities that produce an emotional state that can be measured in minutes, hours, days. You do the activity, think the thought, eat the food and the sensation lasts for a few minutes. The moment the sensation is over, you are out looking for another hit to return you to that heightened state. This is the realm of food, gaming, movies, alcohol, sex, drugs, shopping, adrenaline – I think you get the idea. Searching for this type of fulfilment is a bit of a wild ride; quickly you will start to realise that even in the middle of the pleasure there is a part of you that knows it is only temporary.

What is medium-term fulfilment? These states can be measured in months and years. More thought and effort are required to achieve this type. It comes in the form of education, career, designing, writing, creating, building. Effort and focus of attention are the earmarks of this type of fulfilment. The rise to this state is slower. However, there is no sudden drop off at the end. It is a steady and continuous movement in a direction. There may be a sense of tremendous loss when it has come to the end of its time, like picking the last of your summer crops, selling the house you built and loved, the end of a career or graduating from college. At the end of this 'addiction', you will be required to find another.

What is long-term fulfilment? I think this is the most attractive of all the forms. In saying that, it is the one form that is the most challenging and, in my mind, the most rewarding. The one word that could describe this type of fulfilment is 'legacy'. Knowing that you have made a difference in the world. It is about realising your short existence on earth has had a positive effect on the people around you, or on the world. What is it that you have done with your life that will live beyond your eventual death? This could be as simple as building a better mousetrap, producing an evergreen piece of music, writing a poem or book that will be passed down through time. True, it may take significant time and investment of resources. It could also be thrust upon you by chance. Your legacy could be bringing up children, the future generations who can forge the balance with others and the natural world. Children that are nurtured for their gifts, talents and creativity.

Legacy is about becoming a master so that your apprentices evolve into the masters that continue your skills through time.

Take the time to discover your short, medium and long-term fulfilment objectives. By doing this you will experience a more sustainable and stable sense of fulfilment. Your trip to Mars is just as important as eating chocolate cake!

Where do relationships and love fit into the concept of fulfilment? Relationships can be of the short or medium-term type, depending on what type of relationship it is. A friendship can last for a few hours, or a lifetime. An intimate relationship can be a one-night stand or a lifetime partnership. The love you have for all humankind is a legacy. The default type of 'love' between parents, children and family is a biological and social survival connection.

The illusion of happiness that comes with the condition of someone loving you stands on shaky grounds. Love originates within you, so only being happy if he or she loves you is putting love outside of yourself. How can you have love from another when you don't first own it yourself? First love yourself, then you can share this love with another. External love is not connected to true happiness.

Building fulfilment requires a never-ending cycle of time, energy and resources whereas the state of happiness does not. True happiness is constant and unconditional.

Honour your core values

You've just told someone you don't have time for a weekend cooking class, yet on receiving an invitation to go skiing for the weekend, you drop everything to go. Maybe it's because you love sports, maybe you love being in nature, maybe you love the people you get to hang out with when you go to the snow. Whatever the reason, you place more value in this than joining a weekend cooking class. You prioritise that which you value.

Building a fulfilling life is about honouring your values, doing what is important to you and what makes you feel alive. How do you know what your values are? Ask yourself this set of questions.

1. What is the most important thing to you in life?
2. What is the next most important thing to you in life?
3. And the next?
4. And the next?

These four answers clearly show you what your top four values are. These values determine how you like to spend your time. It sounds obvious but when you're not motivated in your job, you only have to look to your values and you will observe why work is a drag. Often parents visit me with their child, who is failing at school. I ask the child what is important to them and instantly you can see why they are failing school. I recall one set of values being surfing, gaming and reading comics.

You cannot nag someone into doing something that they just do not value. If fulfilment is alluding you, then look to your values and discover what is important to you and do more of that.

> Doing nothing is better than being busy doing nothing —Lao Tzu

If you perpetually find yourself doing unfulfilling activities, occupations and pursuits, ask yourself these questions:

- Am I clear on what my values are and what they mean to me?
- Do I know what activities fulfil me as they are aligned with my values?
- Am I allowed to pursue and do the things that I would like to do?
- What is stopping me doing or pursuing the things that I enjoy?

Closely examine your answers above as these will identify the significant drivers of your dissatisfied state. Did you observe the presence of limiting beliefs? Are there situations or people controlling you?

Teflon and Bugs Bunny

I once worked with a group of students whose theme throughout their training was Teflon and Bugs Bunny. You see, Bugs Bunny is Teflon, nothing sticks to Bugs Bunny. Nothing! Every problem for our Bugs Bunny is always an opportunity for a solution. He has little to no neuroses, and while he does have an ego, it is joyous. Everything about his sense of self is joyous. Why do you think Bugs Bunny is always the hero instead of Daffy Duck? Because Daffy Duck is always so preoccupied with trying to win while simultaneously trying to keep all of his issues under control. Bugs Bunny does not have to do this, so he just wins.

I have a large stuffed toy of Bugs Bunny in my office. It was given to me by that particular group of students. Actually, I have a number of large stuffed toys in my office, another being Winnie-the-Pooh. Winnie was a character referenced repeatedly amongst another group of my students. Now, Winnie-the-Pooh is not especially smart, but because he stays true to his own nature, he is always okay in the end. Meanwhile, all the other characters in his world struggle. For example, there is Owl, who pontificates, always pretending to be wise whilst wearing his scholar's hat. Poor Eeyore always seems so sad. Rabbit is always busy doing absolutely everything while achieving hardly anything. Pooh is just himself, and we often refer to him as the uncarved block: pure, unshaped, naturally powerful. He is perfect just as he is and he is the hero because he always wins. He always wins because he is the one who lives by his own personal rules.

> **It's easy to win when you write your own rules.**

A most important lesson in life. It is impossible to win at a game when somebody else is writing the rules and can change them at any moment.

In life, we tend to put on the hat representing the role we feel we should play within any given family or social group. You may enter a group and feel like the best way to survive is to put on the hat of a wise person and pretend to be wise. It could be that you pretend to be busy or sad or happy. All these pretences are equally as neurotic as each other. Always being in control, always being right, always being the victim or the persecutor – these are just hats that we wear. Wearing a hat and pretending to be someone else is not right or wrong, but is it the life you want to live?

In many cases, the hats we wear represent the coping mechanisms that we develop to keep us safe from our unresolved emotions. If you are always depressed, is that a good or a bad hat? Neither, but it can get rather heavy from time to time, hindering your progress in life. The same applies to the hat of 'always being in control' or the hat of 'being the victim'. If you are pretending to be clever, who are you being clever for? Maybe to make yourself feel better, or maybe for the other people in the group in order to falsely lift your status. Or you could be acting depressed and playing the victim so that other people can come and rescue you. Whatever the hat is, you can choose to take it off.

Let me ask you the following questions:

- Are you that hat you wear, or are you infinitely more than that hat?
- Are you your emotions or are they just part of you?
- How much are you prepared to pay in time, effort, energy and money to keep your hat and negative emotions maintained?
- How much liberation would there be in not wearing any hat at all?

The cost of being fulfilled is that you have to get rid of all the hats you are wearing that are preventing you from being happy. You may be thinking, 'But I am my hat! Who would I be if I was not my hat?' The answer is you would be who you *really* are. You could be your own creation rather than the result of your environment as a seven-year-old. We all have our hats that are unique to our personal experiences. It's up to you to choose whether you take off your hat and find the real you.

Today is the day

Have you ever said that? Today is the day that things change! Said with tremendous conviction, driven by a bellyful of frustration at things just not working out the way you had dreamed they would.

Do you observe successful people around you or on TV and admire how they seem to have it all together: money, connections, health and influence. Highly successful individuals all share a set of common traits. They dream. That is the easy bit that we can all do. Then they plan. Planning is less popular. Then they take action. Okay. Next, they keep taking action. This is even rarer still. Finally, they will change their behaviour to suit the environment. This is the rarest trait of all. This pattern is the simple formula for success. Simple yet to many it is an impossibility.

There are many reasons as to why taking action presents such a challenge, but what it really comes down to is the alignment of your values with your goals. A practical way to tackle large goals is to decide on which bitesize actions would provide a stepping stone to the completion point. These actions or mini-goals then have to be installed into your unconscious mind. The easiest way of doing that is to repeatedly do them. Start with the smallest task daily, and then build on that. Performing the actions in the sun, rain, hail or storm until they become second nature is being on the path of long-term fulfilment.

As a result, you become the actions and the actions become you. It is a little like learning how to walk. In the beginning, it is challenging; after a bit, you can do it. In no time at all, you are walking without even thinking about it. This process works regardless of the type of goal you have set yourself. Again, if it is so simple why isn't everyone doing it? The reason is neural inertia. A person's history of beliefs and habits can pull you in other directions. That is why it needs to be done daily; every time you do the action it becomes just that little bit stronger. A behaviour done once is like a twig, easily broken. Thought or action that is repeated a thousand times is unbreakable. It is also installed in your unconscious, and this is the passage to mastery.

CHAPTER 6

YOU ARE NOT THEM

Who asked them, anyway?

Have you ever been in the situation where someone is telling you what you should do or what you should think when you weren't aware you even had an issue and you certainly weren't asking for their advice? Who asked them, anyway? There can be a feeling of violation when someone jumps out at you and tells you what to do or say or how to be. It's like they are calling out to you that you are not okay as you are!

> **Someone else's opinion of you is none of your business.**

In the work that I do in helping others I first confirm that my client is asking for my help. I verify that they believe they are stuck and that they are ready to receive help right now. I confirm that they are not here because someone else told them they have a problem and need to get it addressed. If any of these checks fail, then I halt the session right there. It would be arrogant and disrespectful of me to continue. When someone tries to force their opinion on you when they were never invited to do so, halt the conversation. Similarly, if you start dishing out advice to someone else when there was no invitation, don't invite yourself! Who asked you?

At times when you observe someone doing something that you believe is negatively impacting them, you might feel compelled to step in and advise, or help. However, it is still not your place to judge whether that person needs help or not. Respecting the other person's model of the world and accepting that everyone is doing the best that they can with the resources that they have is more likely to bring about friendship or a supportive relationship. And most importantly it is their choice to be where they are right now.

Some questions for you to consider:

- 'What am I inviting?'
- 'What am I ready to work on?'
- 'What insights am I asking for right now?'

Thank the people you hate

We are influenced by the people we love and who love us. Equally, we are controlled by the people we are opposed to, or even hate. In fact, I'm starting to think that the ones we hate may have a stronger impact on us than the ones we love. So, thank those individuals that have betrayed you, broken your heart, treated you unfairly. Each of them has given you the opportunity to learn and grow. They taught you many valuable things about you, relationships and the world.

Most people have issues with their parents. Parents place boundaries in our path so we may push against them, making us stronger in the process. If life is handed to us on a platter, there is no struggle and no learning as a result, and when the time arises, and if we do have an issue, we will have no experience and knowledge as to how to handle it. Successful people fall often but just keep getting back up.

Giving up the blame game

Taking responsibility for your choices, actions and then the outcomes is being at cause, likewise owning your emotions and being present with them. But if you blame someone or something else for your pain and dissatisfaction, you are at the effect of something external to yourself. Being at effect means something happened to you without any choice, action or influence from you. When someone criticizes you or hurts you indirectly or directly and you react and place blame on the 'offender' for your 'hurt', then you have placed yourself on the effect side of the equation.

Cause and effect present two possible paths to take in life. When something crappy happens in your life, the questions that place you at cause include:

- How did I make that happen?
- What did I do to create this situation?
- What didn't I do to create this reality?
- How have I chosen to respond or react?

The moment you place yourself at cause, you are empowered to choose a response and initiate change. It is an acknowledgment to yourself that you, your history, neurology, values, beliefs and choices created the event or outcome. Because you created it, you give yourself permission to change the behaviour that got you there, if you wish to.

Living on the effect side of life is when you constantly blame someone or something else for your problems, and you become powerless to do anything about them. You cry out 'Bad things just always happen to me' or, 'People just don't like me' or, 'They are bad influences on me' or, 'It is because of my _____ [insert one or more of these: parents, education, religion, race, age, gender, sexual preference, height, weight, eye colour, I.Q.] that I am dissatisfied.' The list can be endless.

When you live on the cause side of life you are empowered to change. When you live on the effect side of life everything seems to control you and you are full of excuses with the accompanying pointing finger of blame.

A friend of mine was the mayor of Parkes, a country town in Australia. He happened to be the longest-serving mayor in the history of Australia. He said that if one more person sued the council for tripping over a footpath, he would rip up all the footpaths in all the parks. He added that if another kid fell off a swing and the family sued the council, all the park swings would disappear. This is how litigious society has become. We live in a blame culture that's so bad that if there is an unmarked cliff and someone falls over it, the council can be sued.

The more you pull your awareness towards 'being at cause', the more you can focus on what is actually occurring and therefore have the power to do something about it. I will guarantee that in certain aspects of your life, you will be sitting on the cause side of the equation, and with other aspects of your life, you will be sitting on the effect side of the equation. It is almost like a pendulum in that respect: it will swing from one side to the other, depending on what area of your life you are looking at.

One of the common traits of highly successful people is that they are at cause. They place themselves there.

My dad has an interesting saying. 'Robb, if you find yourself in a problem, get yourself out.' Another wise person I know says, 'When you find yourself in a ditch, stop digging.' In rehabilitation programs like Alcoholics Anonymous (AA), the first step is to raise your hand and admit, 'I have a problem, and this problem does not have anything to do with the rest of the world. I am the cause.' It can be difficult to hold your hand up and say, 'I am at cause.' Being at cause also includes whom you choose to hang around with. I have found that when I put myself at cause, the people around me either fall away or they pick up their game.

As humans, we are constantly working out where we are within groups. Are you dominant or passive? If you are forever being dominated or bullied in a situation, the question is what are you doing to allow or encourage that to occur? If you don't ask yourself this, you are at effect and are powerless to change the situation. If I accept responsibility for the predicament I find myself in, I am empowered to do something about it. I'm going to be brutal here and say that if you walk into a situation and someone picks a fight with you, the unconscious dynamic between the two of you caused that to occur. Unconscious cues from body language and vibration are always in play automatically and outside of your awareness. We can learn a lot about the conflict, persecution, victim and bully interplay between humans by observing the predator and prey relationship in animals.

Predator animals including pet cats and dogs will not chase an animal until it behaves like prey. The very action of running away is the signal to the cat or dog that the animal is prey. Up until the point before the prey started to run, the prey was not aware it was prey and the predator was not aware it was a predator. Our little pet chihuahua, Max, demonstrated this perfectly one weekend we stayed on a farm. There was a chicken wandering around the garden who was oblivious to Max, who was watching her intently. Max had never seen a live chicken before that weekend; he didn't recognise what he was looking at. He was observing it closely, trying to determine whether this animal was a predator or prey. The moment the chicken spotted Max, it started running for its life. The act of the chicken beginning to run turned a cute 3 kg lapdog into a killing machine. No amount of Allison screaming at him broke through his trance. Max did catch up with the chicken, but Allison grabbed him before he pounced on it. The chicken 'caused' Max to chase it. The chicken behaved like prey.

I would like to invite you from this point on to ask yourself 'How am I at cause?' when you find yourself in a crappy situation. Your reward is freedom and empowerment to choose your thoughts, your response and your actions from this point forward.

Freedom in responsibility

I had the fortune of knowing a martial arts teacher who had an interesting view on winning and losing. His perspective was that if he left a fight and his clothes were ruffled, he had lost. His reasoning was that if his clothes were ruffled, the battle had changed who he was, and this was unacceptable. Do you get ruffled or perturbed by day-to-day events? If you do, you are allowing the situation and people around you to control who you are, how you feel and how you act. How many times have you lost it because a phone rang at the wrong time? How many times have you been affected by the content of a conversation? You are allowing an external thing or event to control your internal state. It could be your kids, your family, your friends, your partner. It could be a situation, an event, a circumstance. You could be floating along perfectly well and all of a sudden the wheels fall off because something occurs on the outside.

Would you like to be the master or the slave in life? Frequently, we give power away to organisations, banking systems, political systems, medical systems, school systems. All the answers that you will ever need exist in one place right now: inside you. Mental bodybuilding to get to the position of liberated is important because only you are in charge of your happiness. You are in charge of your own clarity. You are in charge of your finances. You are responsible for your actions. You are responsible for finding out where your blind spots are. You are in charge of taking the time to observe any self-sabotage behaviours you might be displaying. When you embrace responsibility, you become the owner of the results of each action you take. You can decide if those results were worth you taking that action or not. If you decide to drop the action in the future, then perfect, move your focus to something else.

The current global economic situation is catastrophic but, in every economy, somebody somewhere makes money. Being adaptable, like a chameleon, to any situation is powerful. During the great depression of the 1930s, a few industries made an absolute fortune: industries involving alcohol sales, gambling and prostitution. Those businesses took people away from the problems they had via an altered state.

The liberated person takes responsibility for their life, or to put it another way they are 'response-able'. This person has the 'If it's to be, it is up to me' approach to life. There is no question of fault; they just look for what they want to achieve, and they take action in a systematic way. A systematic approach is knowing which problem to address first or which step to take first in the direction they desire.

What you are learning right now may seem pretty straightforward, but when you come to start changing your perceptional ability, these foundations are vital. You will get to a point where you will think 'This is so obvious! Why did I not do this before?'

The answer has nothing to do with intelligence or even common sense; it's simply that you didn't understand the process until now.

Purge your fake laws

Inside our heads most of us are hanging on to outdated internal laws on right vs wrong, good vs bad, success vs failure. I use the term 'law' because that's the way we blindly abide to a whole range of life rules without question. The laws outside our heads that run a society evolve over time to reflect the current environment and within context to the parts within that environment. In the same way, the laws that rule your inner world could do with a regular purge of those laws that are outdated. On reviewing your internal laws, you may discover that some have no meaning to you, but they may have had meaning to your parents, teachers or peers twenty or thirty-plus years ago. Each time an internal law pops up, revise it according to these questions:

- What are the positives of keeping this law?
- What are the positives of purging this law?
- What are the negatives of keeping this law?
- What are the negatives of purging this law?
- Can I drop this law?
- Can I create a new instrument to guide me in my desired direction?

Good vs bad

You may think success means that you have to drive a certain car, buy a certain house, have a certain job, earn a certain amount, wear certain clothes or consume whatever material goods the media is selling you at a particular point in time. The moment you subscribe to such notions, you internalise somebody else's notion of what happiness or success means. Young people are tortured endlessly by advertising lures. They're sold promises that people will like them or find them more attractive if they own certain products. I remember being at school over forty years ago and being teased because I wore Amco jeans instead of Levi's! That's the power of advertising. I'm sure you can think of similar examples from your childhood.

As a teenager, you rebelled against many of the family laws in order to become an independent adult that could survive and adapt to your social environment. Do you have any residual outdated laws inside of you from childhood that are mucking your life around today? You are here because of all of the events that have occurred in the past. It is not a question of good, bad or indifferent, it is a question of benefit and relevance within a context at a point in time. Some of the laws that worked for your parents and grandparents may be of little benefit for you today.

Was Adolf Hitler a good or bad person? The fact is that without him, certain technological advancements would never have occurred. The Boeing Corporation was put on the map specifically because of the Second World War. Computing systems were specifically developed to break the German coding systems. That development propelled all computer technology one hundred years into the future. The Motorola Company sold walkie talkies to the US government. Motorola chips were the first chips to be used in all mobile communications devices, which set the standards for mobile phones. Penicillin was pushed forward in leaps and bounds because of the Second World War.

In this way it can be understood that events are neither good nor bad. They have consequences: for every action, there is an equal and opposite reaction. But you may not know the consequences or value for many years after the event itself, because we usually only look for the immediate results.

> A farmer had a son and a horse, and together they ploughed the fields. One evening, a herd of wild horses appeared from nowhere, causing the farmer's horse to break free and run off with them. His neighbour leaned over the fence and said, 'Bad news about your horse running away. You guys are going to have to plough the fields by hand.' 'It may be good, or it may be bad. I don't know,' replied the farmer. A week later, his horse returned with the entire herd of wild horses. The old guy from next door leaned over the fence and said, 'Good deal you have with all those new horses.' 'It may be good, it may be bad. I don't know,' the farmer again replied. A couple of weeks later, the farmer's son had an idea to break in some of the wild horses and sell them to make some money. The young boy fell off one of the horses and broke his leg in the process. The old guy from next door leaned over the fence and said, 'Shame about your son's leg.' 'It may be good, it may be bad. I don't know,' came the farmer's reply. By this point the neighbour thought the farmer was crazy. A couple of weeks later, the army came to town, looking to conscript young men. The young boy could not go because he had a broken leg. Maybe good, maybe bad. Who knows?

You cannot garner the full consequence of an event at the time the event is occurring. You can become imprisoned inside the concept of good and bad; it locks you into a mindset of fear and avoidance. There is really no such thing as good or bad, only the consequences that come from a choice. Teach your children this and you will teach them how to be at cause, the most empowered position to be in when you play the game of life.

Right vs wrong

You may recall I first mentioned the docudrama, *What the Bleep!? Down the Rabbit Hole* in the Possibility vs Necessity section at the end of Chapter 3. In this outstanding film, the concepts of quantum mechanics, perception and reality are discussed. One of the real-life individuals in the film is a priest, and he spoke at a seminar here in Australia. During his seminar, a student spoke up and said he absolutely agreed with the message but that he had no reason to worry about the religious stuff. He stated that he was brought up in a non-religious household so the concepts of good and evil and heaven and hell had no impact on him. The priest responded by asking if he believed in right and wrong and the student immediately said yes, he did. The priest replied, 'They got you,' meaning if he believed in the principles of right and wrong, society's conditioning had got to him.

The concept of right and wrong is a social construct of so-called ethical choices that one can make. This is a complex debate beyond the scope of this book, but simply put, indoctrination gives us definitions of what is right and what is wrong. Animals do not live by these concepts. In the case of the priest and the student, the priest told the student that there was no such thing as right or wrong, but if one is living according to the principles of right or wrong, which are indoctrinations, then one is still living according to a religious dogma.

The principles in this book may have you questioning everything you think is true. You will question all of the rules you live your life by. You see, you cannot measure something without measuring it. But the moment that you do measure it, you must ask yourself what rule you are applying in order to measure it, who gave it to you and who told you it was correct. This is because that very rule may no longer apply and therefore may no longer be true.

> A young girl was cooking a roast dinner for the first time with the help of her mother, who told her that she must cut the end off the meat. When the daughter asked why, the mother said that was just what she was taught by her mother. Out of curiosity, she instructed her daughter to call her grandmother and ask. Over the phone, her grandmother informed her that she used to cut the end off the meat so that it would fit into her small oven! It had nothing to do with the process of cooking.

Sometimes people hang on to rules and regulations because of the ritual of it rather than the practicalities or logic.

At the age of ten, I went to Israel and because it was a Jewish country, I was expecting not be able to buy pork anywhere. Not so! There was pork in all of the butcher shops. When we questioned some of the locals, their surprised answer suggested we thought they were from the Middle Ages. In the 1970s, when I was around eleven, we ended up in Italy, the home of the Roman Catholic Church. Because of what I had experienced in Australia regarding the observation of Catholic rituals to the letter, my sister and I assumed it would only be fish on the menu for Good Friday. We could not have been more wrong! All the butcher shops were open. Even strip clubs were open for business. Times had moved on, but the people who had moved from Italy to Australia had held on to the rituals and passed them down through the generations, regardless of whether they were relevant to the time they were living in. They continued without even really knowing or understanding what the rituals were for in the first place.

Rules and regulations can be insidious like that. Most of what we know and understand to be right and wrong is put in place by the time we are seven years of age by our parents, teachers, other caregivers and role models. This may have been twenty, thirty, fifty-plus years ago. Whatever age you are, you are still operating according to the rules you learned as a small child. In fact, a lot of the things you learn in school, especially pertaining to how you learn, are not particularly useful in real-life situations. In school, if you are caught comparing your answers with another student's answers, it is considered cheating, whereas in business, it is called collaboration or teamwork. At school, if you don't know the answer to a question in a test, you get marked down for it. In business, you just ask someone or research it. The foundation for all education and the real reason school exists is to support and teach godliness, cleanliness, timeliness, discipline and hierarchical order. The purpose of school was originally to train people for factories, not to prepare them for life in the modern world.

CHAPTER 7

THE REAL YOU

What is real?

Your reality, what you believe to be true, is not the absolute pure truth; it can be very far from it. Respectfully, I'm not saying you're crazy. I'm stating everyone is crazy!

Our realities are distorted. If you truly understand this topic, you will never have a problem ever again. By understanding how the brain perceives reality, you will have the capacity to transform the way you experience life. You may discover the problems you are experiencing are because of your perception of what constitutes a problem. The why and how you experience something as a problem is unique to you. A problem may be held in place because of a belief, your values, your purpose or the meaning of your life.

Every second of every day billions of bits of information float past our awareness. As clever as our mind is, it can only process a small percentage of this information, so it will select the parts it will observe and the parts it will ignore. As a result of this process, our brain creates its own version of reality – a reality that is only a minuscule representation of the entire information stream. Each brain being unique creates its own unique representation of the world.

Remember the story of the three girls and the cat? Each of the three girls experienced the same event in a different way. Similarly, if the mind is conditioned for poverty in early childhood, it will in turn search and find information that will support this position in adulthood. Ironically, it will also delete all information that is contrary to this unconscious belief. This process creates an inner reality that can be vastly different to the true external world.

Our perception of the outer world is a biased representation; a tiny subset of the world external to us. We see what we expect or have been trained to see. Our memory filters all information passing from the outside to the inside. Likewise, we hear what is expected or have been conditioned to hear.

As a youth I had low self-esteem. I would have done anything to have a girlfriend in school, but I knew with total conviction that no girls were interested in me. As a result, there were none to be had. Many years later, I discovered that several girls had approached me at school. However, in my version of reality these conversations didn't happen, so I didn't recognise their interest even when it was right in front of me.

Personal filtering system

How you behave is determined by the characteristics of your mind-filtering system that is unique to you. The components of a filtering system include your beliefs, values and conditioned behavioural traits. Simply put, your financial, relationship and health situations are the results of how your mind innocently filters, distorts and deletes incoming information passing from your external world to your brain and body. These filters can work in harmony and in sync with each other, or in many areas can be the source of conflict and pain.

There was an interesting American game show whereby the central idea of the show was giving homeless people a million dollars and finding out what would happen. Every single one of them blew all the money and all the contestants ended up back on the streets. The reason? The values and beliefs of the contestants were so out of line with the concept of having money that they simply could not handle it. Real-life statistics reflect just how influential a person's set of values are, as it is their silent internal compass. Up to seventy per cent of lottery winners are bankrupt within five years of winning the lottery! The fact is, having that kind of money requires a different set of skills, beliefs and values. Securing the money does not guarantee that you will have the set of skills, beliefs and values to keep it. Under normal circumstances, people with that kind of money acquire it over time, which gives them the training required to handle it. Giving a large sum of money to a person without this knowledge and skills is a bit like handing a Ferrari to a toddler.

When life is not travelling in the direction you desire, then observe your personal filtering systems. I've presented a set of questions here for you to help you identify which pieces of information are unconsciously being thrown out the window. The information that is not being weighed in by you holds a crucial piece of the puzzle, so it's important to retrieve it. Each question set is organised under each filtering type.

Beliefs

- What belief do you hold that keeps this problem in place?
- What would happen if you dropped this belief in order to dissolve the problem?
- What would happen if you held the belief and dropped the problem?

Values

1. What is the most important thing to you in life?
2. What is the next most important thing to you in life?
3. And the next?
4. And the next?

Now reflect back on a current problem and ask yourself, is the problem only a problem because someone else wants you to be or do something that does not align with your values?

What would happen if you only expressed yourself and did things in accordance with what was of value to you?

Memories and Conditioned Responses

- How are the qualities of this problem similar to something that has happened in the past in the same or a different situation?
- How are the qualities of this problem different to something that has happened in the past in the same or a similar situation?
- Does this problem seem like a repeat of a problem you have encountered before?
- Can you identify one thing that stands out to you as the linchpin to the problem? If pulled, would it dissolve the problem?
- Are there associated triggers that are unrelated to what is happening in this conflict today? An example of this might be if you're in the car with a friend, and a song plays on the radio that you associate with a massive fight with your ex-boyfriend, and you suddenly become aggressive towards your friend.

- Can you see a connection of this problem you are facing today with another problem that is either current or historical?
- What emotions are associated with this problem that you recognise from a time in history?
- Can you see any common thought pattern or behavioural pattern underlying any of your persistent problems, including this one?

Be open to change. If you're expecting events to repeat, then they are likely to do so because that is what you are looking for in the streams of information flowing past your consciousness.

Allow the dynamics of relationships to change. Allow personalities to change, allow situations to change. Allow yourself to change in how you interact in situations. Allow yourself to express yourself differently.

Past history is a good predictor of future behaviour, but only if you choose this and only if you consistently cherry-pick the same information from the billions of available answers streaming past your awareness every second of every day. Be patient with yourself and be kind to yourself. Know that one new piece of integrated information can move mountains.

Your unique reality

Your outside world is a perceived construct. Your perception creates reality, and your responses and experiences are consequences of this interplay between perception and reality. For example, if each time you pat a dog it bites you, you could form a perception that all dogs bite, which leads to fear being triggered whenever you see a dog. On the other hand, another individual who loves dogs and grew up with them would have a completely different perception. Hence their reality and behaviour towards the dog would be completely different to yours. This concept is simple but the way it is applied in all areas of your life is revealing.

What are some of the perceptions that have been created by your memories and determine your current behaviour? Most of the driving perceptions would have been put in place before the age of seven: sense of self-worth; social hierarchy; your adaptive ability; your sense of belonging. Realise that you are no longer a seven-year-old and you are free to shed those shackles.

The next time you go out into the world, start to observe how your reality bends and flexes depending on your perception. Consider how you interpret events and what meaning you assign to them. Notice how your emotions change depending on what meaning you assign to each event. How much more power do you have to direct your destiny with this knowledge? Each and every one of us lives in a unique dream world. My question is, are you choosing to experience a nightmare or a nice dream?

Things are not what they seem

A long time ago, I was involved in a TV commercial as a stunt actor. The experience made me realise how much of what you see on television is a fantasy. The actual commercial that was shown on television was between thirty and forty-five seconds long, but the filming took nearly four and half days of me being wet and cold in a river! There were thirty-five people in the crew, even though you only saw three people and a dog on the screen. Similarly, our news is perceptional and a fantasy. We have a solid media configuration in our society known as 'If it bleeds, it leads,' meaning that the most dramatic and provocative stories are given preference, to ensure viewers keep tuned in. So, what do we see? We see a distorted perceptional view. Consistently, the media's aim is to deliver information that triggers an emotional response, regardless of accuracy, because we are more likely to watch that type of content. If our primary emotions of fear, anger, love and lust are involved, we will watch it to get that emotional fix.

This is the basic framework for what I teach. Let me take you into Alice's rabbit hole for a moment. Many of the beliefs you have held to be true for the majority of your life are about to change. This includes issues surrounding who you are, the roles you play and even where you fit on the gender spectrum.

I will give my life defending our rights as human beings, but on the basis of gender, I will not. To see where I am coming from you would first need to understand one of the more discreet purposes behind the women's movement. Who were the main supporters in the USA for the women's movement? Industrialists. Because the industrialists realised that if women came into the workforce it would increase the total number of people in the workforce, which meant more people for the industrialists to sell to. More employees in the workforce meant more income tax for the government. The government was happy because they collected more income tax, and the corporations were happy because they knew it would grow the economy. One group that was quietly opposed to the women's movement were the women who were married to successful men, because it meant there would be more competition in the workplace. When we are presented with something, we always have to ask what is behind it. What is the political agenda? What is the social agenda? Many of the beliefs that we hold to be a solid truth are often more fluid than that. Things are not always what they seem.

The inside is the outside

> A mother brought her diabetic child to see Gandhi. She said, 'My child eats too much sugar, please help me.' Gandhi replied, 'Bring the child back in two weeks.' Unsure why Gandhi couldn't help her child in that moment, the mother left and returned two weeks later. Gandhi pulled the child aside and told him it would be best if he stopped eating so much sugar. The boy agreed that he would do his best to cut back on sweets. Confused, the child's mother asked, 'But why didn't you just say that two weeks ago?' Gandhi replied, 'Two weeks ago I had an obsession with sugar. I needed the time to see if I could cut back myself.'

We but mirror the world. All the tendencies present in the outer world are to be found in the world of our body. If we could change ourselves, the tendencies in the world would also change. As a man changes his own nature, so does the attitude of the world change towards him. This is the divine mystery supreme. A wonderful thing it is and the source of our happiness. We need not wait to see what others do. —Mahatma Gandhi

Gandhi knew he had to give up eating sugar so he would be 'walking his talk'; his behaviour and his words would be congruent. At an unconscious level, the child would observe the congruency and the message would be powerfully persuasive.

Anything occurring outside of you is an extension of what is happening inside of you. If a person has clutter in their surroundings, you can guarantee there is clutter on the inside. If someone is highly critical or judgemental of others, this is an extension of their inner world. If there is violence on the outside, something unpleasant is going on inside. If someone is manifesting depression or confusion on the outside, then what do you think will be going on inside ? You see, the inside is the outside and the outside is the inside. This is one of the foundation tenements of Wicca or witchcraft. The Wiccan saying, 'As above, so below', is a perfect illustration of this. The Wiccans believe that whatever you think about, you bring about in real life – that is, your thoughts are a reflection of what's going on outside of you, which means that what's going on outside is a reflection of your thoughts.

Feng Shui is an ancient Chinese practice based on art and science. Its aim is to balance the energies of any given external environment to ensure the health and wellbeing of the people inhabiting that space. A similar principle to the Wiccan ideology mentioned above. The masters in this area are so well versed and experienced that they could enter your abode and could do a psyche profile on you based purely on your environment – and it would be accurate.

> **Look within for the answers.**
> **As the inside is the outside.**
> **As above, so below.**

CHAPTER 8

INSTANT INFLUENCE

Tidy language

One of the objectives of my teachings is to get you at least on good terms with your unconscious mind. Ideally, you will make it your best friend and work as a team. If you continually burn resources arguing with yourself, how can you get anything constructive done? How can you live your dream life?

Start observing your inner commentary. How much chatter do you do in just one hour? Is it positive and supportive, or negative and judgemental of yourself and others?

Imagine someone has a knife to your throat and you are yelling abuse at this person. Imagine calling them all sorts of names and telling them what a pathetic person they are, all while they hold your life at their disposal. In the same way, your unconscious mind has the ability to kill you, yet you are abusing it and giving it a hard time by calling it ugly, stupid, weak, dumb, fat and lazy. You are abusing the part of you that holds the power of your life in its hands. I am amazed at the patience of the unconscious mind. It will put up with years of abuse while holding the blueprint to your health and wellbeing. Do you agree with just how tolerant that part is, inside you? Can you imagine being as forgiving as that part?

One of the fastest ways to transform your life is to change how you communicate with yourself. The following guidelines will give you a new appreciation for the power of some commonly used words.

We all know and use the word 'try'. The word 'try' holds the essence of potential failure. The sentence 'I will try to be there' means 'I will possibly be there, either fail or succeed'.

'Hope' also equates to a potential failure. 'I hope it will work out' really means, 'Okay, I'll try, but I'm a bit wishy-washy on it'. Similarly, the word 'wish' has no solidity to it.

The conscious mind will not register the word 'don't'. The conscious mind only has the ability to 'do'. Think of the sentence, 'Don't think of a blue tree.' You have to hold the conscious image of a blue tree in your mind in order not to think about it. Imagine a parent saying to their child, 'Don't run in the house.' You have just asked the child to create an image of running in the house. This image drives behaviour.

In summary, remove these watery words as much as possible from your inner talk and your conversations with others: not, try, hope, wish. This sounds easy enough, but in the beginning it may be tricky. To a large extent we all speak from our unconscious mind, in other words, from our old habits of thinking and feeling. To effect change, it is first necessary to observe our language in action. This is where your friends can be of great assistance, much like the work colleague in the 'not peanut butter again' joke at the start of this book. Ask your friend to alert you every time you use one of these words. Think about the words you use to describe yourself and the choices you make. Do you use phrases such as, 'I hope to', 'I will try to', 'I wish I could'? Your brain registers your words and says, 'Okay, I'll try, but I don't have to succeed' or, 'I hope to, but of course it won't happen'. How about you say this instead: 'It will be done.' Feel the difference? Brains love clear directions, just like using a GPS. You never put in the location of all the places you aren't interested in going. Go directly to your destination. Start using 'I do', 'I am', 'I can', and motivate your brain. Here are some more tidy language examples:

- I will be on time (instead of: I will try to be on time)
- I exercise every day (instead of: I will try to exercise every day)
- I am successful (instead of: I will try not to fail)
- I am smart (instead of: I don't think I'm stupid)
- I have faith that it will all work out in the end (instead of: I hope it will work out in the end)
- I eat healthy food (instead of: I hope I can eat healthy food)
- My assignment is completed on time (instead of: I hope I won't be late with my assignment)
- I am curious (instead of: I will try to be curious)
- I know I can figure it out (instead of: I wish I could figure it out)

Do, or do not. There is no try. —Yoda

There are two other commonly used words that are important to learn about in terms of their inclusion in statements and how meaning can change dramatically depending on whether you use one or the other word. The first of these words is 'but'.

When I say, 'I love you, *but* you annoy me,' the position of the placement of the word 'but' effectively negates the 'I love you' sentiment. If your intention is for the 'I love you' part of the sentiment to pervade, then restructure your sentence like this: 'You annoy me, *but* I love you'. The word 'and' placed strategically can be used to create an inclusive sentiment in the above sentence. You could say, 'You annoy me, *and* I love you'. To recap, placing 'but' in your sentence can be used to negate (deny, decline, exclude) something that you are describing in the sentence after your placement of the word 'but'. The word 'and' can be used in place of 'but' if you would like to ensure it is clear that what you are describing on both sides of the 'and' are inclusive.

'Can't' is another word I'd like to bring to your attention. Using the word 'can't' takes you to a disempowered state. Know the difference between you 'can't' and you 'won't', or 'don't want to'. When you don't want to do something or you won't do something, then be clear in your communication and say what you mean. Your practice is to use the word 'can't' only when something is not physically possible to do.

The simplicity of using your words with care and with volition will gift you the ability to express yourself clearly and fully with ease. Start today by observing yourself using these pivotal words: try, don't, should, hope, wish. After observing yourself for a number of days then begin to swap out the *failure*-structured sentences with the *success*-structured sentences. Also, begin to notice your use of the word 'but' and decide whether the word 'and' is more appropriate.

You shouldn't should

'Should' is an interesting word. An old teacher of mine used to say, 'Robb, you shouldn't should on yourself. Only use the word should if you are in possession of a time machine!'

The word 'should' by its very definition implies that if you had known what you know now about some point in the past, you could have done things differently. It is only through the experience of doing it then that you are here right now, therefore, you can't should on yourself.

As we have discussed in the Tidy Language section above, words have an effect on neurology and on how you behave. If you catch yourself saying 'should', give yourself a smack in the head, metaphorically speaking, of course!

The word 'need' is also interesting. We often use the word 'need' when it's actually a 'want'. How many times a day do you use the word 'need' when it's actually a 'want'? How might your unconscious mind react when so many of your so-called needs aren't met? Your mind and body will become a lot more relaxed if you relax on the number of needs.

Some tips. Instead of using 'I should…', 'I need to…', 'I must…', 'I have to…', use 'It would be nice to…', 'It would be enjoyable to…', 'It would be beneficial to…', 'I would love to…'

Most likely the shoulds, needs, must dos, must haves, have tos come from the conditioning in your childhood years. A liberating feeling is to surrender the expectations that no longer serve you.

> **Once you surrender expectations then all that is left is what is important to you.**

Now for the good and the bad news. Some individuals have taken my courses and have gone on to become multi-millionaires. Other individuals have gone from having high-paying executive positions to throwing it all away for the purpose of following a dream of growing vegetables. One of my students, Karen, was earning about $5,000 a week. Karen was working so hard that she had no relationship, no social life and no prospect for doing anything else other than working. I am happy to say that she now lives down the coast in a small house on a farm. She works one or two days a week in the city and she has two kids with a man that she adores. She was only doing the job because she thought that was what she was supposed to do after getting her degree. She thought that as a woman, she had to look after herself. Now, Karen has found a healthy middle ground for herself.

> **Make the choice to love what you are doing today or change it.**

I have another story about a student called John, who just wanted money. He wanted to buy himself an F1 Ferrari and a fifty-two-foot yacht. I know it was a fifty-two-foot yacht because his neighbour's was fifty-one feet! John attended a ten-day course with me, and he was well on the way to buying his Ferrari when he was diagnosed with leukaemia. He came back to me for one-to-one help. What had happened was that his unconscious mind had become sick and tired of his lifestyle, which involved all work and no play and was seemingly driven by his ego. We had a serious conversation and we negotiated that he took at least one day off a week and did some exercise. Nearly eight years later, he runs marathons. He did not buy the Ferrari, but he sold his large city house and bought a place in the country. He still lives and works in the city, but he is making the transition from city to country life. His quality of life with his wife and kids is significantly better and he is happier. He is still a financially wealthy individual, but at the time when he became sick, his unconscious mind was warning him to halt his ego-driven lifestyle and live his purpose.

Can your unconscious mind kill you? Yes, without question. So, every day remember two important things: you are in charge of your decisions and goals, and there is no room for 'should' in the construction of your dreams. Your goals exist to create meaning in your life, and only you can decide if they support your dreams or not. Make the choice to love what you are doing today or change it.

Sphere of influence

When concentrating your focus on an area with a level of concern and with emotional investment, you expect something out of it or intend for something to happen. When your push or pull on the area is not making any difference, or the outcomes are not being achieved and it's an uphill battle, then it's time to stand back and look at your sphere of influence. It's not about the level of expenditure of your resources, it's about what influence you have on the area you are vested in. When you have no influence on the area, then no amount of concern and angst and effort will make any difference. Persistently worrying and ruminating on this area of concern with no influence produces a neurotic state of mind.

Having a circle of concern mismatched with the circle of influence would be equivalent of you as a heterosexual female entering a male homosexual bar with the intent of attracting a sexual partner. No amount of primping and preening and learning how to attract the opposite sex will lead to the outcome you desire. Your sphere of influence would be next to none. Another example would be trying to convince your local council to instal a skate ramp when ninety per cent of the local residents are over seventy-five years old. Your keenness (concern) for a skate ramp for your child and his friends does not give any weight (influence) to the decision by council. However, if you happen to be one of the council board members, well, now you have a sphere of influence.

In the area where your concern overlaps with your area of influence lies the possibility of change. If you have influence in an area but no concern, then no problem. If you have concern in an area and no influence, then how quickly will you recognise this and change tactics? You could look at ways to achieve a greater sphere of influence or you could surrender and find areas where you can make a difference.

Being continually concerned with something with no influence to change it will cause you feelings of:

- Pain
- Powerlessness
- Futility
- Despair
- Hopelessness
- Anxiety
- Stress
- Depression

Changing your behaviour is about being aware and catching yourself trying to push a cowpat up a hill with a toothpick. Make life easier and happier for yourself. Put effort in where it matters to you and where you know you can make a difference.

Problem

We are constantly bombarded with media messages and images of war, famine, assault, murder, pandemics and world disaster. We have little to no influence over these things but because many of us are concerned and feel the need to act, it leads us to a state of disempowerment and feelings of hopelessness.

Solution

An empowering solution is to reduce your areas of concern to coincide with your ability to influence. I am a big fan of media fasting! If it's really important, someone will tell you. If you see me looking at a newspaper, it's usually for the comic section in the back. What is reported in the news is simply someone else's point of view cloaked with propaganda, and follows the dynamic relationship cycle pattern that is described in the Three of Me section in Part IV. Why do people feel like they absolutely must watch the news when it's all doom and gloom and there's not a damned thing you can do about any of it? Guess what: The news is about drawing in viewers to create a bigger market for advertising dollars! Drama sparks your adrenaline and adrenaline can become an addiction. Are you addicted to drama and having problems? Or are you already finding solutions, and have influence in the circle you are connected with?

When you focus on that which you have influence over, it grows. When you focus on that which you are concerned about but have no influence over, you diminish your resources to influence. You end up disempowering yourself and create internal hopelessness.

> **Feed your circle of influence, this is where your true power is.**

There is an old Native American folk tale about a young boy who had anger issues.

> 'Papa, I am having problems with my anger,' a boy admitted to his grandfather. The grandfather replied, 'Anger and love are like two wolves that live inside each and every one of us.' The boy responded, 'Which one is the strongest, Papa?' The grandfather said, 'Well, that depends on which one you feed.'

The message here is that if you feed your circle of concern, it will grow. If you feed your circle of influence, it will grow. The irony is that if you focus on your area of influence for long enough and are effective in doing so, it can actually start to overlap with those items you were concerned about before and had no influence over.

Focus on your area of concern, not your partner's, not your family's, not your friends'. If you are concerned about the rest of the world, first get your own shit together. Focus on your fulfilment. I am talking about long-term fulfilment here, not short-term highs. If you are living a happy and complete life, this will affect those around you positively.

There is selflessness, selfishness and super selfishness. Which one do you think I advocate? Super selfishness! Super selfishness implies that I would never take an action against another that in the long term would harm myself. This is not equivalent to the popular saying 'Do unto others as you would have done unto you'.

Selfishness implies that I might think I can get away with it. If I carry out an action against you that then comes back and harms me, then I am the fool. What I'm interested in is Super Selfishness. Anything I can do to promote you and get you to a happier and more productive place ultimately helps me. I can influence you right now with my words in this book, but I cannot influence what is going on in any world conflict. Yet, if I influence you positively, it has a positive effect on your life. Reading the paper, watching the news and getting upset and emotional about all of the ills of the world are counterproductive. By focusing on those things that you can positively influence – yourself, your relationships, your health and your finances – you'll then have the resources to expand your area of influence to be of assistance to others.

CHAPTER 9

WHEN TRANSFORMATION BEGINS

The point of release

Kirk, Spock, Bones and the master hypnotist

In the movie *Star Trek V: The Final Frontier*, the crew came across a character named Sybok who was a master hypnotist. Sybok asked the people that he crossed paths with to share their pain with him. His philosophy was that in sharing the pain, they would become free. When Sybok encountered the crew, the first of the three main characters he came into contact with was the doctor, otherwise known as Bones. When asked to share his pain, Bones envisioned an image of his dying father in front of him. His father had an incurable disease and was in terrible pain. As a doctor, he had simply switched off the machine to stop his father's pain. Three months later, a cure for the disease was found. This was the pain that Bones was carrying around with him. Once he shared this with Sybok, Bones felt free. The freedom and relief he felt was phenomenal. Bones then told Spock and Kirk what had happened and encouraged them to release their pain too.

Spock was up next, and if you've ever watched any of the *Star Trek* movies, you will know that he is the geeky, logical character of the three. The image that came up for half-Vulcan, half-human Spock was of his Vulcan father looking at him as a newborn baby and saying, 'Hmm, so human' and then rejecting him. Spock's reaction was to say that yes, he understood that as a Vulcan, his father would reject him for his human qualities. For him, his logic had enabled him to overcome all of his childhood issues and he had no residual pain.

When Sybok came to Captain Kirk, his response was to tell Sybok to bugger off. As far as he was concerned, he was his pain. For him, his ability to lead and to solve problems was directly related to his pain. He threatened Sybok and told him not to come anywhere near him!

> **Some things we need to let go of, some things we need to rationalise and some things we choose to keep.**

Do you relate to how each of the characters handled their problem? One let go, one rationalised the problem and the other utilised it. I think that each and every one of us would benefit from being able to do all three of those things. Some things we need to let go of, some things we need to rationalise and some things we absolutely must keep. What do you think would happen if we removed all traces of pain from our life? There is a good chance that you would do nothing. You may just lie down and die. That drive to overcome and to achieve is in fact, a bit of pain. Without pain, you would fail to breathe. Breathing itself is triggered by carbon dioxide irritating the nervous system to the point where you are forced to take a breath in. The pain you need to keep is the pain that drives you in the direction of what is meaningful to you. The pain you need to get rid of is the pain that stops you from going in the direction you desire.

The turning point

To actually live in the moment is one of the highest manifestation skills you can ever achieve. When we are not living in the moment, we are projecting our history or an imagined future, or acting out of automatic habit. Habits occur because of historical memory. If we only do things because of history and habit, we become blind to that which is occurring in the present. If you have the prevailing ability to live in the moment, your level of awareness is heightened, allowing your observation and reaction times to speed up significantly. Living in the moment is the sharpest form of sensory acuity and it is from this place we can redirect our life.

Observing what is truly occurring in the moment gives you the ability to take the appropriate action. Knowing that each moment is different to the last opens itself up to a possibility of a different outcome. Our memories, habits, beliefs and values can hold a problem in place.

> Two monks were crossing a shallow stream when they noticed a lady struggling to cross in her long dress. The older monk said to the lady, 'Climb on my back. I will carry you across the stream.' The younger monk was shocked because their faith forbade physical contact with females, but he said nothing. The lady climbed on the old monk's back and he carried her across the stream and set her down safely. The lady thanked the old monk and went on her way. As the two monks continued on their journey, the older monk

> noticed his companion appeared troubled and asked him what was wrong. The young monk said 'Master, I am puzzled by your action of carrying the lady across the river when it is a contradiction to our teachings.' The Master replied, 'My dear disciple, I stopped carrying her hours ago, but you are still choosing to carry her.'

When you replay a painful memory repeatedly or imagine a negative future, you are choosing to build an ongoing cycle of unnecessary suffering. This suffering is built on fantasy. When I talk about fantasy, I refer to a memory or an imagined future that does not exist right now in your current reality.

The true and greatest freedom exists only in this moment. This moment is the only time that you can choose how to respond and decide on what action you'll take; you have ultimate freedom to pivot in any direction, accept any invitation, learn a life-changing lesson, gain a new perspective.

Do you catch yourself when you say things like 'I'll be happy when…', 'I'll relax if…', 'I'll do this when…', 'I'll feel like this if…'? The conditions you place on yourself that are completely outside your control say a lot about how you encourage suffering. You may feel rewarded or receive satisfaction from suffering and self-flagellation. Hey, I'm not knocking your persuasion of masochism, but are you using the suffering as an excuse or a distraction or a means to draw in sympathy? By choosing a perpetuating cycle of suffering and pain, you may discover you fall into the role of victim as your default coping mechanism. Again, The Three of Me section in Part IV explains the role of victim playing.

Joe, one of my clients, asked if I could help him resolve his epileptic fits. He had heard that I had helped a handful of clients cure their epilepsy. Joe's fits occurred sporadically throughout the day and night. Joe was now fifty years old and hadn't been able to work since he was twenty-five due to his condition. He had been living off a disability pension for twenty-five years. We discovered that there was an unconscious resistance to letting go of his condition. We discovered he was fearful that if he recovered, he would lose his pension and he had no skills to find a decent job. The turning point for Joe was when we negotiated with his unconscious mind that he could retain his epilepsy between the hours of 1 a.m. and 2 a.m. The epilepsy during the day ceased. The wonderful thing is that Joe became well enough to study bookkeeping and eventually found a job as a bookkeeper.

An interesting and powerful process that we observed in Joe was the holding on to a problem because of a perceived gain or avoiding a perceived loss that was strongly connected with the problem. The problem was held in place until we addressed the perceived loss; we gave the unconscious mind a satisfactory solution to the perceived loss. The unconscious mind is so powerful in its protection of your survival. This dynamic is called secondary gain.

Another example of secondary gain is a smoker not being able to let go of smoking because of the fear of losing his closest social network. Yet another example is an obese woman who is in danger of having a heart attack or stroke, but does not want to lose weight because her husband loves her size. Can you think of any problems you have that might be held in place by secondary gain? There is no right or wrong in maintaining a problem because of secondary gain, but it is valuable to see the whole context if nothing else to give you a sense of relief and empowerment. A circumstance or situation is a problem when you perceive you are not actively exercising your freedom of choice to choose it or change it.

> **Only when we are sick of our sickness shall we cease to be sick.**
> —Lao Tzu

Now that we are nearing the end of Part II: Building Solid Foundations, I'm wondering what insights you've discovered about yourself. Did you arrive at a new level of understanding around areas of your life that were once troubling you or confusing? What resolutions did you come to? How has your self-awareness expanded? Have you discovered any of the old problems have been downgraded to learnings that you can now see past? How did you go with building your solid foundations in readiness for the next part of the book: Transformation?

The gateway to transformation is about first making room for it. Maike Sundmacher, one of my wonderful graduates who has been a trainer, coach and writer for over a decade, will guide you to the starting gates of transformation.

Making room for change
By Maike Sundmacher

I once had a lengthy conversation about life with my good friend, Annie. I know what you think: that sounds like a terribly large topic. Well, it is, but it wasn't. You see, Annie was a clever and jovial lady, but there were some aspects about her life she didn't enjoy. I assured her that most everyone experiences these aspects.

Annie pressed on. 'You don't understand, Maike,' she sighed, 'I know I shouldn't complain, but there are some things that I simply don't enjoy about myself and my life. I want to lose weight and I do so well for a while and then I go back to my old self. Everyone thinks I am so successful, but sometimes I feel like a total loser.'

I sat back and listened as she continued.

'And then there are times when I get really dissatisfied. I want to feel content and happy, but I look around and I don't find much that surrounds me that I can get enjoyment from: neither things nor people.'

'So, you want to change?'

Her response was a single but firm nod.

'Okay, then. Maybe before you can change, you need to make room.'

'Room for change?' Annie queried.

'Yes, exactly. Room for change,' I confirmed.

Since Annie's eyes remained that certain kind of blank that indicates that although my words had arrived at their destination, they had not sunk in at all, I told her the following: 'Well, Annie, imagine you inherit a beautiful house. There it is: standing on a hill, tall, straight and full of magnificence. As you move closer, you realise it might need some fixing up: the doors creak, the windows have cracks and the paint on the walls – once fresh and bright – has faded. You enter a corridor and where once hung colourful pictures of happy times, only dark spots remain.

'There is dirt. There is dust. There is broken furniture. In fact, some rooms are so full of stuff that you can barely enter. There is no space left – especially not for new things, different things. Yet, you walk around and admire the house's solid foundation, the history it carries and the time and effort it has taken to make a home of it. Yes, it needs some work but oh my goodness – it has so much potential. It just needs some cleaning, it just needs some dusting, it just needs some clearing.

'So, you sit down on an old, wobbly armchair and start rocking back and forth, pondering over how to turn this house into something you love and adore. Where do you start? What do you want it to look like? How do you want to feel about it? How do you seek to feel living inside of it? What to keep and what to leave?

'Closing your eyes, you start planning and designing your new dream place … you know it'll take work; you know it'll take time. You know it won't always be easy. But you also know that it'll be well worth it. You are ready for it. You're up for the challenge. So, you get up, make the first step and get to work.

'Now imagine you are that beautiful house. You do stand tall, straight and full of magnificence, yet there are some aspects that need renovation. So how do you remodel that house into something you love and adore?'

Annie contemplated my words for a while. There was silence, but the comfortable kind. The silence that doesn't need to be filled with unnecessary chatter or clutter. At last she said, 'So what you're saying is that I should take stock of what works for me and what doesn't and then let go of the stuff I no longer need?'

'Bingo!'

'But how do I do this?'

The conversation continued late into the night. Maybe a bottle of wine (or two) went with us and maybe a pack of chips as well. But that's another story…

Like Annie, most people have aspects in their lives that worked well for them for a while but that have outlived their use-by date. Some of us even have aspects that never worked for us and yet we cling on to them as if our life would end if we stopped doing just that. The key is to identify these aspects and muster up the courage to let go of them so that we have space for something new.

Too many people claim they are ready for change, that they dream of a different life, that they seek out something new whilst they remain sitting on the sofa they bought in their twenties, drinking the same brand of beer their dad introduced them to when they were a teenager.

As humans, we love living in our comfort zone where things might not be fantastic, but they are also not too bad either. So, we sit on our sofa, talk about how great life would be if only ... whilst firmly holding on to everything we've accumulated over the course of our lifetime: possessions, beliefs, decisions, habits.

Of course, sometimes we are not yet ready to let go of the old and welcome the new, and sometimes we just don't know how to start. And that's okay.

However, if you – like Annie – really seek change, if you really wish to create something new in your life, then a brilliant first step is to make room for change: clear your mental, emotional and physical space. Declutter. Get rid of stuff that doesn't serve you any longer. Take out the trash. This way you create room for something new to come into your life. Whether, in a second step, you deliberately design it or simply let yourself be surprised by the universe, that's up to you.

Usually there are four broad categories that are full of clutter: your environment, your relationships, your behaviours and your thought patterns.

Your environment

Let's start with the one that I personally consider to be the easiest: your environment. Most of us own clothes we no longer wear, books we no longer read, trinkets we no longer like and gadgets we no longer use. Get rid of them. It's as simple as that.

Just get started: room by room or drawer by drawer, whatever is easiest for you. Getting rid of stuff doesn't necessarily mean throwing everything away: you can fix it, donate it, sell it or give it to someone who can appreciate it.

Go for it. I can wholeheartedly assure you that once you get started, it's hard to stop. The feeling from a clutter-free space that's ready for something new is addictive.

Your relationships

Let's look at an area that is slightly more complex: your relationships. Which relationships bring you joy, inspiration, motivation and make you feel good, and which ones don't?

Most of us have friends whom we have known for all eternity, but somehow things between us don't gel as well any longer. Maybe the relationship has passed its use-by date. Yet, we cling on to them or tolerate them just because … well, because why?

It is liberating to ask yourself from time to time which relationships positively contribute to your life and which ones don't. Write down the specific parts you like about your preferred relationships, like the activities you do together, the topics you talk about, how you feel and behave being around that person. Then do the same with those relationships that are energy-drainers for you. I am pretty sure you'll find patterns quickly.

Take it from there. You might decide it's time to leave some people behind and make room for new ones or change the relationship to keep the person in your life but assign to them and the relationship a different meaning and level of importance.

Your behaviour and thought patterns

You can start working on these yourself: awareness is key. Start with a brainstorm:

- Recall one significant time in your life that you behaved in a way you didn't appreciate or enjoy. Write it down without judgement.
- Then recall what you were thinking about yourself and the world at that time. Write these thoughts next to the behaviours.
- Have a look at your list and identify any patterns you can observe.

Now, repeat the steps above, only this time start with your thoughts first and the behaviours that followed. Chances are that the lists will be similar, but you might be surprised by how a change in sequence can influence the outcome.

You can repeat the above exercise for any behaviour and thought pattern you would like to address.

When Annie did the exercise, she noticed that every time she didn't succeed the first time she tried something, she called it quits and then put the activity or behaviour in her mental 'too hard basket'. After berating herself for a while, she then proceeded to convince herself that it wasn't for her anyhow and that her life would not be any better if she succeeded.

Because of that, Annie's too hard basket had grown over the years with a proud collection of behaviours she deep down wanted to change but hung on to because she had tricked herself into believing that it was easier that way. What a great con-woman she was! This was a cycle that most certainly needed to be broken.

Fortunately, eliciting this pattern and shining a light on it helped Annie to break it. Since it was now in her awareness sphere, she could spot these quite easily and intervene. 'Stop!' she would yell. 'I am choosing a different approach this time.'

The key is to identify unwanted thoughts and behaviour and replace them – slowly but surely – with ones that are more aligned with your vision of yourself and your life. Whether you metaphorically smash them with a hammer, thank them for whatever their positive intention was before you let them go or write them all out and burn them in a ceremonial bonfire, that is up to you. The main thing is to stay alert, be proactive about yourself and your life and to give yourself the time, encouragement and space to change.

So now what?

Whether you have decluttered one part of your life or all, be proud of having taken action. Celebrate!

'So that's it?' I hear you ask. Well, of course not. Just like you shower every day to get the dirt off your body and just like you regularly dust your shelves, you need to regularly declutter. Self-development and growth are a life-long journey. It's a joyful and exciting journey.

And always remember you are that beautiful house. You do have a solid foundation, a history, and it took time and effort to create you the way you are. Every possession, relationship, behaviour and thought pattern to date has had some significance in creating the you that you are today. This needs to be appreciated. And whilst some of these still serve you well, it's time to say goodbye to others.

So, get up, be creative, make the first step, get to work and, most importantly, have some fun with it. Just like you, I wonder what the redesigned house will look like. Let the transformation begin.

PART III

Transformation

PART III IS ABOUT transformation principles and techniques. You will learn about the power of questions and the art of solving problems at many layers. I will share with you a set of hand-selected self-help change techniques that can be applied to any challenges you are facing today or in the future. I've included three techniques to release any enmeshed fear. Entering Part III with a sense of curiosity and adventure will stand you in good stead. On completing this part, you'll have made some fundamental mindset changes that will open up freedom of choice. You will have increased clarity about who you are and will have learnt how to harness affirmation and contemplation techniques for accessing an empowered and fulfilled life.

CHAPTER 10

THE POWER OF QUESTIONS

The answer is in the question

A question opens the mind. A question opens a gate. A question is an invitation for an answer to come forth. When you ask a question, it is a premise of possibility whereas a statement fixes information in place, the information that is already in your memory; it puts a wall up to new information.

The way you frame a question, the way you construct the question, the intention of the question and the context of the question will lead you to the answer. You have the answer already inside you because you were able to construct the question. Often the answer is already in plain sight but you may have overlooked it because of your beliefs diverting you away from it. As you continue reading through this part of the book, you'll be strengthening the muscle of answering your own questions. The key is to leave judgement at the door and humour the answer that rises up no matter how odd it might seem at first. Remember this isn't about being comfortable, it is about finding answers and solutions to your puzzles. There is comfort in being uncomfortable because if it was comfortable, you would know it's your old pattern, and we are seeking and finding the new ideas that flow into your awareness when you open the door with a question. In time after the initial uncomfortable clunk, the truth becomes the pathway to perpetuating self-actualisation.

> **Society today doesn't want to be uncomfortable or inconvenienced by the truth. The secret to the most rewarding path is in persistently seeking your truth. —Allison Low**

Internal negotiations

Finding a win-win solution when you're trying to resolve a disagreement or a conflict with another person seems like a fair proposition. But have you ever noticed that you can be having a conflict inside yourself, where one part of you wants to go in one direction and another part of you wants to go in an opposing direction? It's like when you're on a diet to get fit, but there is a part of you that loves eating a big piece of cake every day.

Surprisingly, the real problem is not that there are two opposing forces which are a construct of your own mind – it's the indecision and the suffering that accompanies them. Also, the inner voice telling yourself you must have both can create further stress. The words 'must', 'should', 'got to' used in your sentence provide strong clues.

The conflict arises between two seemingly opposing areas because: one or both of the areas are not of true value to you but are of value to someone else or in accordance with societal expectations; one or both are being used as a distraction or as an avoidance of an emotion or situation. Each area will hold a valid reason for being present because they each represent protection or a coping mechanism, regardless of whether it seems logical or not. The resolution of the internal conflict will follow one of three paths:

there will be one true clear winner; both sides of the conflict may drop away as you may discover they are not truly important; or in listening to and processing both sides of the conflict, you reach an internal agreement on how to satisfy each need. Ultimately, there is one winning direction and that is through negotiating a win-win arrangement. Often, contemplating what each part is trying to express resolves the conflict.

In our natural state, our body is in harmony and it behaves for the good of the whole. What you say is important to you, but the reason behind this may have been corrupted. The questions below can help you discover this corruption. Grab yourself a piece of paper and a pen.

Recovering your true answers from your unconscious mind is the focus of this next exercise, as this is where your internal compass resides. Answer as quickly as you can, as this excludes critical thinking and reasoning.

Exercise

Write down your two-sided conflict clearly and succinctly. Also write down what you feel when you think about the conflict.

In the questions below, you can substitute anything for A and B according to a conflict you are having between two areas (e.g. A = eating cake, B = getting fit).

Step 1: Discovery
1. Who said A is important, is it you or someone else?
2. Who said B is important, is it you or someone else?

If you answered 'someone else' for either question 1 or 2, then you can skip past the rest of this exercise since the conflict resides outside of yourself.

3. What are the benefits of A for you? What is the positive value behind A?
4. What are the benefits of B for you? What is the positive value behind B?
5. How do the benefits of A and the benefits of B relate to each other?
6. How do the benefits of A and the benefits of B not relate to each other?
7. If A is not of true value to you but is being used to suppress emotions (avoid fear/pain)? Yes/No
8. If B is not of true value to you but is being used to suppress emotions (avoid fear/pain)? Yes/No
9. Are you using A to distract you from something you don't want to feel or see? Is it a coping mechanism?
10. Are you using B to distract you from something you don't want to feel or see? Is it a coping mechanism?
11. Are you using A as an excuse to do/not to do something?
12. Are you using B as an excuse to do/not to do something?

Now that you've answered the set of twelve questions above, check in with the previous conflict you were having. Have you come to a win-win arrangement? If one or both of your areas have been identified as a coping mechanism, then the underlying issues to what you're protecting yourself from can now be addressed.

Step 2: Collect your value set

1. What is the most important thing to you in life?
2. What is the next most important thing to you in life?
3. And the next?
4. And the next?

Now think about A and B in relation to your values. Which area aligns most closely with what is most important to you?

Step 3: Check-In

Now, say out loud:
1. 'A is more important to me than B.' Notice the feeling that accompanies this statement.
2. 'B is more important to me than A.' Notice the feeling that accompanies this statement.

Now refer back to your notes and say out loud what your original conflict was. Look for the old feelings when you say this statement. How have you resolved the old conflict? Does it feel different, or has it resolved completely?

CHAPTER 11

RELEASE IT

Empty out

Can't see the trees for the forest? Can't see the wood for the trees? Is it time to do some clearing so the light can flow through and you can see clearly what there is, and what there isn't?

Many of us have a nice story that props up our problem. You know, the one that begins with, 'Well, when I was ten, and so and so did this and then this happened to me and I felt like this and man that was {frown} {grimace} {sad} {angry} and then when I was twenty, the same thing happened to me {frown} {grimace} {sad} {angry} and so and so did this and I was feeling like this and isn't that just unbelievable and what do you think of that?'

The one thing I know for sure is that this story is real for you. The bits that make up your story, the recollected memories, are real to you. To be blunt though, it does not matter if they are real or not. What is important is the answer to the question: Is this story helpful to you? If keeping this story happens to be part of how you get noticed, how you receive attention, then ask yourself this. Are you your stories? Or are you more than that? Would you prefer freedom from this thing? Would you like to be done with the old story now?

One great way of getting everything out of your system is to talk it out or write it out. Emptying out is the opposite of saying 'I don't know'. A by-product of emptying out is opening up awareness and increasing your clarity.

If you love to talk, then ask a friend to sit with you and guide you through this next exercise. The perfect friend for this exercise is someone you trust, you feel comfortable around and who will be able to remain quiet throughout by not giving advice or judging. They are simply there to elicit the empty-out process for you.

If you're not so much into the idea of emptying out with someone's help, then you can do the same exercise just as well by doing the prompting yourself and talking out loud, in your own mind or, by writing down your flowing thoughts.

Empty-out exercise

Find a comfortable seat in a quiet space. Place both feet on the floor and take one deep breath and let it flow. Take a moment to check in how you feel when you think about the problem. Where do you feel it in your body? If you were to give it a score of intensity from one to ten, what number would you give it? Whilst the information flows out below, your focus remains fixated on the peripheral visual area to the left and right. As you are concentrating on the periphery you may or may not fall into a gentle trance of learning. It may happen now or later on as you talk or write.

Exercise

Talk (or write) out everything that comes to mind about a problem. This can be crazy, irrational, nonsensical; whatever comes out is perfect. This is not about making sense. It's about emptying all the stuff out relating to the problem. Empty it all out. No commentary or double-thinking or judgy stuff … just let that proverbial poop flow out. Remember as you're emptying out to be focussed on the right and left areas of your peripheral vision as if in a trance.

When you've finished, ask:

1. What else is in there related to this problem? Or is it all gone? If it is all gone, skip to Step 10. If not, proceed to Step 2.
2. Talk (write) out everything else that comes to mind about the so-called problem. Keep going until you are completely empty of all things to do with this problem.
3. Then check, is this problem gone? If not, move to Step 4, otherwise if it's all gone then move to Step 10.
4. Is this problem yours or someone else's?
5. What would happen if this problem disappears?
6. What wouldn't happen if this problem disappears?
7. What would happen if this problem remains?
8. What wouldn't happen if this problem remains?
9. What would happen if you simply let this problem go?
10. Check if this problem is not actually a problem but an opportunity to learn something.
11. How do you feel? Do you feel at ease? If so, go to Step 12. If not, repeat from Step 1.
12. Done

Take a moment now to check in how you feel when you think about the old problem. Has it shifted somewhat? Or has the feeling shifted altogether? If you rate the feeling on a score of intensity from one to ten, what number would you give it? Has this number changed from the beginning? Let's continue on your path of transformation.

Presence in body beats presence of mind

Absence of body beats presence of mind is the usual saying, but this saying leads us in the wrong direction of solving a fear pattern stuck in your nervous system or your psyche. Your unconscious mind is the voice of your body. When you have a pattern of fear, worry, anxiety or trauma that is stuck in a loop and cannot exit, no amount of telling your body to stop it will have any lasting effect. When there is a program of fear running under the surface, you display a heightened sensitivity to the slightest of conflicts or challenges in your everyday life. Flying off the handle, at the drop of a hat, and so on.

Having a massage in the hope of relaxing and relieving this pattern of fear works for all of a few hours or, if you're lucky, a few days. The only permanent way out is through knowing how to communicate with your body, your unconscious mind, using the language it understands. In this context, being present in your body will beat the presence of your conscious mind.

Unwinding

The unresolved problems in your life have associated feelings that become enmeshed in your unconscious mind. At the core of these feelings is the primary emotion of fear. It is this fear pattern that has come to resemble an automatic alarm bell that you seem to have no control over. Our bodies, our nervous systems hold memories of an old fear even if the cause is no longer present. I recall a time when one of my clients had an anchored fear of answering the phone. Weeks before she came to see me, she had received a phone call in the middle of the night that brought some devastating news. Her brother's lung had collapsed, and she was told he may have only hours to live. At the time she was on the other side of the world and there was no way she could make it back to his bedside within a week, let alone a few hours. That one phone call for my client set up a binding association trigger of immense distress, panic and helplessness. This is called a negative anchor. What transpired after this phone call was endless nights of insomnia with an anticipation that the next phone call would be more bad news. Anxiety began to invade her waking hours, too. Each and every time the phone rang, it would trigger a cascade of intense emotions for her.

In your own life, can you think of any negative anchors that have been invading your psyche? In my clinic space, I solve these anchors with various hypnotic techniques in a one-to-one setting. Because it is unlikely you will get to sit in my clinic space, below I've set you up with some powerful self-help tools so that you may move through these fear states with ease.

Many body workers are attuned to working in this area, and the key to resolving the old fear held in the body is to know how to regulate the vagus nerve (the nerve that carries signals from the brain to the digestive system and organs and vice versa). After sustained exposure to or an intense experience of fear, the vagus nerve function can become impaired. Post-traumatic stress disorder (PTSD) is one clinical condition that overtly displays this vagus nerve impairment. PTSD is often associated with soldiers returning from a war zone, or civilians caught up in conflict or in a catastrophic natural disaster. However, trauma can be a result of physical or psychological abuse, neglect, abandonment, the loss of a loved one or loved pet, an accident, ongoing bullying at work, being stalked, online harassment, poverty, a severe fright (sometimes leading to the onset of a phobia), chronic illness, or growing up with a parent suffering from a mental illness, whereby the parent was emotionally unavailable or extremely intense and erratic.

The same disaster, circumstances or event that is experienced by two people will not affect both people in the same way. We all have our unique ways of coping and responding. Some of the common symptoms of a dysregulated vagus nerve include: anxiety, depression, mania, hyperactivity, panic attacks, stress, worry, confusion, demotivation, memory issues, back pain, headaches, gut issues, blurred vision, dizziness, thyroid issues (feeling hot or cold), breathing issues, inflammation, autoimmunity, weight issues and sleep issues.

Even though a trauma may have been trapped in your body in your early childhood, regulating the vagus nerve to release the trapped emotions can be achieved in under thirty minutes. I discovered a powerful set of vagus nerve-unwinding exercises presented online by a craniosacral bodyworker by the name of Sukie Baxter from Whole Body Revolution®. Sukie would love to share these exercises with you here.

Unwinding practice
With thanks to Sukie Baxter for inspiration and guidance.
25+ minutes

For your very first unwinding, complete the exercise below every second day for one week. A day's rest in between each exercise day gives your body time to integrate and equalise. Repeat the exercise anytime you feel the need to unwind your vagus nerve in the future.

What to expect from completing the exercise? Relaxation, freedom of body movement, release of pain, clarity of mind, and the resolution of previous related vagus nerve-deregulated issues.

When completing these exercises below, be gentle with yourself and take your time and be guided by your own body on how much and how long you can perform the practices.

Find a quiet room and wear loose-fitting clothes.

Step 1: Shake it out

- Before sitting down, from a standing position shake out your hands and your legs for about one minute.

Step 2: Somatic meditation with eyes open

- Sit down on a chair, or on the floor in a comfortable upright position. Spend a few minutes bringing your attention to the sounds and sights of your surroundings. What do you notice? Where is your attention drawn to? What are the colours, textures and shapes of things in your surroundings? Begin to wiggle your toes and notice what it feels like.
- Shift your attention to your body. What is the sensation on your skin? What are the overall feelings of your body? What do you notice? With eyes remaining open, without judgement or commenting, go within now and scan your body and observe where there is ease and where there is tension or where there is little sensation or where you notice stronger sensations. What is the quality of your breath? Is it slow, fast, deep, long, shallow, even or uneven?
- Now take a moment to discover your connection of the outside world to your inside world. Observe the quietest sound in your surroundings, and as you hold on to that

sound, what do you notice about the sensations you felt in your body before? Are they the same or shifting? Do you notice any new sensations in your body that were not noticeable before?
- The key to releasing tension and stuck emotions is for your senses to be aware of the now, so that your body becomes synced with the reality of the now.
- Now start to move freely in any way that feels good. Be led by your body.

Step 3: Neck tension release

- Sit comfortably upright on a chair or on the floor.
- The diagrams below illustrate the body positions I'm about to explain. Use them as if looking in a mirror.
- Starting with the right side (Diagram A below), place your right hand on the top of your head, right elbow pointing to the side, and then tilt your head towards your right shoulder so that your ear is moving closer to your right shoulder.
- Now move only your eyes so they look up to the left.
- Keep your eyes in this position and hold for thirty seconds or longer.
- Ideally, you will hold this position until you notice a sigh, yawn or swallow. Sometimes you hear your belly grumble as things start to shift. This indicates when the body has released the vagus nerve.
- Check in with how you feel. How has the tension released in your body? What do you notice?

Now repeat on the left side (Diagram B below)
Take a break if you need to between sides.

Diagrams for Neck Release Exercise – the way to use the diagrams is to imagine you're looking into a mirror. The first image below is your right arm up. The second image below is your left arm.

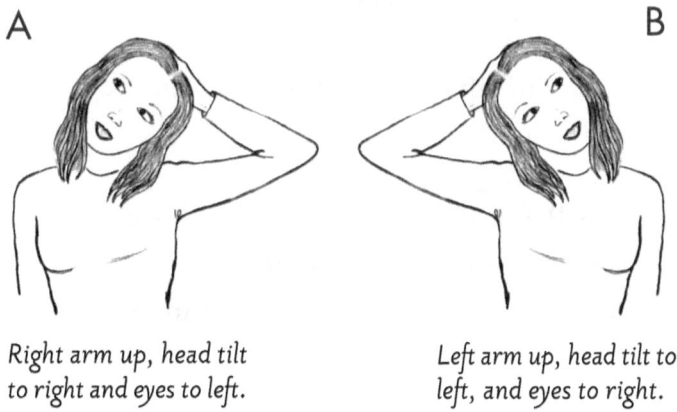

Right arm up, head tilt to right and eyes to left.

Left arm up, head tilt to left, and eyes to right.

Step 4: Rib cage release

- Sit comfortably upright on a chair or on the floor.
- The diagrams below illustrate the body positions I'm about to explain. Use them as if looking in a mirror.
- Starting with the right side, place your right hand on the top of your head, right elbow pointing to the side, place your left hand over the right-hand side of your ribcage. Refer to Diagram A1 below.
- Move your right ear towards your right shoulder. Refer to Diagram A2 below.
- Bend through your ribcage on the right-hand side to form a C-shape. This movement is subtle.
- Now move only your eyes so they look up to the left.
- Keep your eyes in this position and hold for thirty seconds or longer.
- Ideally, you will hold this position until you notice a sigh, yawn or swallow. Sometimes you hear your belly grumble

as things start to shift. This indicates the body releasing stuck emotions (energy).
- Check in with how you feel. How has the tension released in your body? What do you notice?

Now repeat on the left side (Diagrams B1 and B2)
Take a break if you need to between sides.

Diagrams for Rib Cage Release Exercise – the way to use the diagrams is to imagine you're looking into a mirror. Diagram A1 and A2 below is your right arm up. Diagram B1 and B2 is your left arm up.

Prevention is always the best medicine. Responding in a balanced way to your environment and healthy processing of emotions is the key to a regulated vagus nerve. Resolving a perpetuating life problem at the core is the best self-care action you can take. If you haven't managed to deal with your stuff just yet, then you can fall back on this powerful unwinding exercise to reset your nervous system.

Sukie's self-help exercises are based on the work of Stanley Rosenberg from his book *Accessing the Healing Power of the Vagus Nerve*. Rosenberg's vagus nerve therapy is built on Dr Stephen Porges's polyvagal theory. If you'd like to learn more from Sukie, do an internet search on Sukie Baxter, Whole Body Revolution®. I haven't included website links to contributors within the book because over time website addresses change. I have included Sukie's current contact details on our website: www.gdlife.co/booklinks

Fast freedom forward

In this section I've designed two methods to help you achieve relaxation and inner peace. Practising both methods is encouraged when you sense your nervous system is unbalanced (you feel suppressed or wired), or your emotions are stuck, or your vitality has waned.

Tap out the intense stuck emotions

Tapping is a process of engaging particular energetic pathways in your body by lightly finger-tapping on particular points on your body, usually your face and head for practicality purposes. The points of interest to you here will be those that achieve the smoothing of the flow of energy, which is the main principle of

Traditional Chinese Medicine. You may have heard of EFT and TFT: these are popular tapping modalities that are utilised by natural and energy therapists worldwide.

I have designed a simplified tapping sequence specifically to help you to resolve suppressed or intense emotions. Everyone can benefit from these exercises, even if you don't consciously feel you need them.

Before beginning the exercise, familiarise yourself with the diagram below. These are the three points you'll be tapping on shortly with either middle finger and in the order referenced. A is between your eyebrows, B is under your eye (either eye) and C is between your nose and top of your lip. You'll be using this tapping pattern in the exercise below.

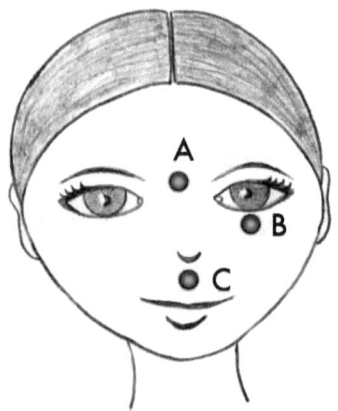

Tap it out exercise

10 minutes

Find a quiet place and a comfortable chair to sit in.

1. Pick a problem that is triggering fear (or any other intense emotion) and one you'd like to resolve. Ask yourself, are you one hundred per cent ready to dissolve this problem right

now? Is this problem yours? If you answer yes to both questions, then proceed. If not, come back later when it is time to resolve a problem that you are currently experiencing.
2. What is the story you tell yourself about the problem behind the emotion?
3. Hold it in your mind.
4. Now focus on the feeling in your body as you think about the story.
5. Where is the feeling located? Describe how it feels.
6. As you focus intently on the problem, lightly tap on point A five times, point B five times, and point C five times. Complete this pattern for three rounds whilst continuing to hold your mind's attention on the problem. Breathe normally.
7. Think of the problem and feel the feeling (if you can find it), and continuously tap on point A whilst you roll your eyes first to the right and then to the left, and then roll them in a big circle in a clockwise direction (ensuring your eye rolling is smooth without skipping any sections). Breathe normally.
8. Repeat Step 7 above except roll your eyes in an anti-clockwise direction instead.
9. Now search for the old problem, old story and old emotions. Can you find them, or have they disappeared? Repeat Steps 2-8 if the old problem is not yet gone. If you can't find the old problem, you can choose to repeat Steps 1-8 for any other problem you wish to dissolve.

Fast fear fix

Fear is behind every emotion that we label as negative. I use the word negative here not to describe something bad or broken. In this context I am using it to describe a state that is impacting the quality of your life and your level of freedom. You can choose to keep your fear in place as it may be considered a protection from a perceptional predator. Fear is the driver behind anger, guilt, shame, sadness, grief, stress, anxiety, depression and addiction. Fear is a natural part of life; it is biologically coded within us. Do you know what you are afraid of? By now, you may have learnt how you can live a fulfilling life despite fear appearing every now and then, by knowing how to respond to it in a healthy way. Have you learnt how to troubleshoot it if it's robbing you of the good life? The key to fulfilment is freedom of choice as opposed to being stuck in a pattern of fear with no exit point. When your triggers for fear control your behaviour – freeze, run or fight – where is the freedom in that?

When fear is suppressed and the underlying triggers for the fear are not resolved, then more and more energy is required to keep it under the water. What is the mechanism of fear? The infographic at the beginning of this chapter illustrates the pathway of unresolved hurt, pain and fear. Failure to address the causes behind these emotions will lead to depression and then to dissociation. In the previous section, Presence in Body Beats Presence of Mind, you learnt how to regulate your vagus nerve.

I have another powerful method to share with you that transforms negative emotions.

In the 1970s, Dr Richard Bandler, the co-creator of NLP, described the building blocks of human reality as submodalities. When we experience irrational fear, the building blocks have been corrupted or disorganised. The exercise below steps you through a reorganisation of building blocks in order to dissolve stuck emotions such as fear, anger, sadness, or any other strong emotion that is negatively impacting your function and fun.

Fast fear fix exercise

10+ Minutes
Find a quiet place and a comfortable chair to sit in.

- Once again, pick a problem that is triggering chronic fear (or any other negative emotion) and one you'd like to resolve. Ask yourself, are you one hundred per cent ready to dissolve this problem right now? Is this problem yours? If you answer yes to both questions, then proceed. If not, come back later when it is time to resolve a problem that you are currently experiencing.
- Tune into this problem and notice what it feels like in your body and where it is located. Write this down, as it's a

record of your baseline that you can refer back to at the end of this exercise.

Use your imagination for the following steps.
1. You are sitting in the projection booth of a movie theatre and you are about to play a movie. You are the only person in the theatre.
2. It's time to play the movie of your problem up on the big screen in black and white at double speed with uplifting music. Halfway through your movie enters a cartoon character called Mo. Mo packs up your problem in a hot air balloon and then counts backwards from ten to one. Once Mo reaches the number one, he releases the hot air balloon. It floats higher and higher and eventually reaches outer space, where it dissolves into a million stars.
3. The movie ends with the stars twinkling as a symbol of new wisdom.
4. Take three conscious, relaxed breaths and look down at your feet. Do you have shoes on? (This is another break state. It allows your brain to reset in readiness for the next part of the exercise.)
5. Now focus as hard as you can on trying to find the old problem you chose to dissolve above.
6. Run the movie you just played, except this time run it backwards, in colour and at normal speed. Once you are back at the beginning of your movie, turn off the projector.
7. Take a moment to find the old emotion. Has it disappeared completely?

If there are any remnants of the old emotion, then ask yourself to locate the feeling when you think of the old problem. Which way is the feeling running? Run the feeling in the opposite direction of this, faster and faster whilst you count to ten. Now repeat Steps 3-8 until you have reached a state of emotional freedom.

CHAPTER 12

REDEFINE IT

Framing

The skill of framing comes naturally to some without needing any extra help from a book. I am unsure where the word framing originated from, but it bears a close resemblance to the idea of a picture frame. A picture on the wall can look cheap and unappealing depending on what frame the picture has around it. A frame can transform the picture style, perception of quality and the level of appeal. When you change the frame, the perception changes and therefore the meaning changes. Below I'm going to walk you through reframing, pre-framing and understanding other viewpoints.

Reframing

Mastering the skill of reframing is handy, especially because it's so easy to use in any conversation with just about anyone, particularly with yourself. I tend to have fun with it and to a large extent, it is the stuff of humour. It also happens to be a quick way to get around mindset blocks and it works well in everyday conversations. Reframing is a simple method of getting a person to look at a situation or problem in a different light using language. Reframing is the art of changing the meaning of something by presenting the same qualities of the situation or problem, but within another context or with a reference point switched around. The easiest way to understand reframing is by studying some examples using some fictitious characters.

Tom says, 'I hate paying so much income tax.' Jerry can respond with, 'At least you are earning good money.' (Same outcome but a positive meaning.)

Amy says, 'I can't stop eating chocolate.' Jo responds with, 'At least you're getting in some tasty antioxidants.' (Putting a positive slant on eating chocolate without changing the behaviour.)

Bruce says, 'My boss is always yelling at me.' Sheila responds with, 'It's a good thing he notices you in a big way.' (The behaviour is still the same, but the meaning of it has changed.)

Marge says, 'My daughter keeps stealing money from my wallet.' Homer responds with, 'It could be worse – she could be stealing from my wallet.' (Same behaviour but different reference point.)

For a problem to be a problem, it has to have a neurological boundary. The moment a problem is reframed, you are metaphorically moving the outside of the boundary, thereby removing the perceptional barrier. The situation goes from bad to good quickly as it is seen in a new light.

One thing to bear in mind before attempting a reframe with someone other than yourself is to first ensure you have built up rapport, as you might get hit over the head if you come across disrespectful.

Here's an example that originates from Dr Richard Bandler. An angry father brought his daughter in to see Bandler, complaining about how stubborn she was. Bandler started giggling. The father, confused, asked what he was laughing at. Bandler apologised and said, 'When I was in college, I was somewhat of a hound dog in that I used to chase a lot of girls. There was one type of girl who, try as I might, I could never get into bed. Stubborn girls!' The angry father left Bandler's office with his daughter in tow, realising his problem had been reframed.

The behaviour of the girl did not change, but the context of her behaviour was reframed, leading to a change in her father's attitude towards it. Imagine if you had the ability to short circuit any situation so that the person complaining about a problem was able to accept a new way of looking at it.

Nothing is ever as it seems at any given moment in time. If someone says A is equal to B and you simply buy into that, then you are doing two people a disservice, them and yourself. There are infinitely more possibilities than A equals B.

I might be going to hell because I did a seriously cheeky thing to my partner, Allison. I don't know what came over me; I just couldn't help myself. I'm a little reluctant to tell you because of what you might think of me, and one of the first principles I encourage is to respect the other person's model of the world. I guess I'm only human and I make mistakes too. The outcome of my action ended well for all, but if it hadn't, I might not be telling you about this. Here goes.

Allison and I went to Fiji on holiday a few years back to relax and do a bit of diving and snorkelling. Allison had just obtained her first level of certification for diving whereas I had been diving for forty years and had recently graduated as Master Diver, Technical Diver, Rescue Diver and Wreck Diver. The morning of our first dive, we had to sign in and, as we did, Allison asked the group dive leader what was the plan for the day. 'We are going to start with the Beqa Lagoon, then progress down to the wreck,' he said. Well, Allison stopped him right there. 'Wreck, what wreck? I'm not going diving on any wreck!' At this point, I jumped in and said to Allison, 'Are you scared of the giant octopus that lives on the wreck?' Instantly, she said 'There's no giant octopus on the … oh … you bugger!' You see, she knew what I had just done as she was midway through her answer.

I'll explain how this special type of reframe works. I reframed Allison's fear of the wreck by swapping out her fixation on it with an object that I knew was ridiculous. The moment her mind rejected the new focal object of the octopus, the fear collapsed. Think of it like this. Initially, wreck and fear were linked together. Then wreck was substituted by giant octopus. But fear and giant octopus didn't go together in her head so the fear dropped away. Sneaky, I know. So, what happened next? Allison and I completed the entire dive, including the wreck, with a sense of excitement and enjoyment. You'll be happy to hear that there was some consolation to what I did: she did gain considerable mileage from that story by telling numerous students and clients about that cheeky side of me.

A lot of comedy originates from the structure of reframing. Humour is immensely powerful and often jokes – black comedy – are developed soon after serious and sometimes tragic incidents. While jokes about death or disabilities may be in poor taste, we need to remember that a thought travels through the nervous system and can stimulate strong emotions. By changing the path of this thought with a reframe, we can change the emotional response easily and effectively. Finding the black humour in tragedy can help some personality types accept what has happened and move forward.

My advice regarding reframing is to practise and have fun. You will quickly see how beneficial it is to you and those around you. Start observing in your conversations who uses reframing naturally and how this transforms the conversation.

> Man suffers only because he takes seriously what the gods made for fun. —Alan Wilson Watts

Pre-framing

Pre-framing is the art of swaying an outcome by using a carefully selected framework of words or sentences. A pre-frame leads the recipients' thoughts or actions in a particular direction. Let's look at the following sentence: 'The next section you are going to read will be long and boring, but hey, it's part of the curriculum, so it has to be done.' What do you think this sentence is doing? It is *pre-framing*. What would your mind be filtering for at this moment in time? It would probably be looking for something else to do, and fast! On reading the above statement, your mind would expect boring and long and you would already be filtering out the interesting bits.

Let's revise that statement to put a positive spin on it yet retain the accuracy. 'The next section is quite involved, but there is a diamond in there. It might take a bit of time, but once you find it, you will understand the real magic in all of this.' Said in this way, the statement sets up your mind to be curious in looking for that diamond, you expect that this will take some time, but now, this is the stuff of magic, not boredom.

The title of a book, book chapter headings and book introductions are good examples of pre-reframing what is to come. Introducing a friend to another friend is also a pre-frame, by setting up the representation of who that person is. Pre-framing is constantly being carried on in your mental chatter; in the conversations you have with yourself. When you're setting yourself up for outcomes before you enter that future, are you setting things up in a positive way or are you sabotaging your future fun and enjoyment? If you are spending time on pre-framing your future, then creating awesome pre-frames will set you up to filter a future of awesome.

Greater than three viewpoints

When you're having a conflict with someone or an organisation, it is clear that the other party has a different objective to you and perceives the situation differently. The conflict often comes with an array of emotions including fear, anger, stress, anxiety, frustration, hurt, sadness and so on. These emotions cloud an objective view of the situation and, because rationality is out the window, so is any potential resolution.

A path to a resolution involves getting a perspective on the other side's viewpoint. The only way you can do this is to first suspend the emotional charge.

> Rocky Clutz was an ex-boxer who did his best to work in a bar owned by his ex-promoter and run by a manager. Rocky did not work for money; he worked for alcohol and slept on the premises. Rocky was not doing well and was living a hard life. One Sunday morning, after a particularly rough night of fighting, the manager noticed there was blood all over the footpath, so he sent Rocky to go and clean it up. Meanwhile, a man called Morris was driving a car down the road towards Rocky. He swerved to avoid a head-on collision with another car and mounted the pavement as a consequence, pinning Rocky against the wall and killing him instantly. The car that Morris avoided was being driven by a lady called Molly. Molly was a single mother who tried to avoid colliding with a third vehicle that was coming toward her by braking. Unfortunately, her brakes did not work in that moment, causing her

> to swerve and almost collide with Morris. Molly was trying to avoid being hit by Lucy. Lucy was a young lady who was driving with wet, freshly painted fingernails while smoking simultaneously. She dropped her cigarette onto her new nylon skirt. She was trying to retrieve the cigarette at the moment when her car almost collided with Molly's car. Lucy had newly painted fingernails because the owner of the sex shop she worked in had required her to do some modelling and had asked her to have her nails painted.

Now you know the sequence of events that led up to the accident, the question before you is what caused poor Rocky's death? Think about it for a minute…

Below is a diverse array of answers, each from a particular viewpoint.

- The coroner might tell you the cause of death was multiple injuries sustained following impact with Morris's car.
- A town planner might say it was due to a lack of median strip between opposing traffic lanes.
- Anti-sex shop campaigners might say it was all Lucy's fault because if she was not working in the sex shop, the whole thing would never have happened.
- The anti-boxing league might blame the years of boxing that led to Rocky having brain damage as a result of multiple head injuries, preventing him from doing other types of work.

The potential list of answers is endless and none of them is right or wrong. It depends entirely on each person's perspective and the context of how they relate to the world.

When you step out of your position and become the observer, you can be anywhere in perceptional space. You begin to see that there are multiple possible answers to any question or dilemma. There is no single right or wrong answer to anything. Each side of a conflict is right from their own perspective.

New perspectives exercise

Think about a current conflict or argument you are experiencing with another person or group. For the purposes of this exercise, let's use the name 'Mad Mouse' for the person or group you are having a conflict with.

1. Imagine Mad Mouse standing in front of you. What do you notice in yourself, what are the feelings?
2. Imagine floating up to the ceiling (leaving all emotions on the floor) and observe the interaction between yourself and Mad Mouse from this neutral position. What do you notice when you look at these two drongos?
3. Now float down into the shoes of Mad Mouse and look back at yourself. What do you notice? What is Mad Mouse thinking and feeling about you and the conflict? Does Mad Mouse see a conflict at all? In what way is it different to your view? Why do you think Mad Mouse holds this view?
4. Now float back up to the ceiling and touch it before floating back down into your own shoes. Look back at Mad Mouse. What do you notice? How has the conflict shifted? Or has it been completely diffused? What new perspectives have you now collected? How has this harmonised the connection?

> **Never get in a fight with a crazy person. An onlooker may not be able to tell the difference.**

Quadrants of change

Cartesian Logic sounds pretty daunting so that's why I've renamed this method here to Quadrants of Change. There are four discrete information storage areas of your brain we can examine by using a specific type of questioning to help you wade through the noise of your thoughts and make a decision. The idea of Cartesianism was first introduced by the French philosopher René Descartes in the seventeenth century.

Exercise

1. State your problem clearly. E.g., 'I am unsure whether I would like a lover.'
2. Then run through these questions that are designed to clarify each of the four discrete information storage areas:
   a. What would happen if you did have a lover? {affirmative}
   b. What would happen if you didn't have a lover? {inverse}
   c. What wouldn't happen if you did have a lover? {converse}
   d. What wouldn't happen if you didn't have a lover? {non-mirror image reverse}

It can be more powerful if someone reads out the questions for you and you answer each one in turn. When you run through the above four questions you'll find that some are easier than others to answer. The questions that are more difficult or near impossible to answer are the most powerful because they hold the hidden gold. They are the areas of your awareness that have not been accessed before.

You might be wondering how a simple question can give you an answer that you were previously completely blind to. You may have spent days, months, years on trying to get a clear answer. What happens neurologically is that the question directs you to access an area of your mind that you might have never looked in otherwise. Just before that question, the area that stored the answer was not accessible because you didn't have a pathway known to you in order to retrieve that information. The question is equivalent to navigational instructions to an area on a treasure map. The gold is found with one of the four instructions. It's your lucky day; you get all four instructions, so you will always find the treasure. The answers are always within you; sometimes they just need navigational assistance from someone else.

CHAPTER 13

CREATING FULFILMENT

Respect each other's model of the world

Every person is the way they are because of their experiences, their memories, values, beliefs and strategies. These things make up their internal reality. Their entire history is what has brought them to the point where they are now in their life. When you respect another person's model of the world and not try and force them into your way of thinking, you actively understand they're doing the best that they can with all of the resources and knowledge available to them. You are acknowledging what they are doing or have been doing makes complete sense to them. Do not insult people by calling them names or insisting you are right and they are wrong. Remember, there is no such thing as right and wrong, only choices. In any case, the moment you start to insult the person you are trying to communicate with, the relationship changes to being adversarial, which is counterproductive.

Disrespecting another person's view of the world also prevents you from finding out why the other person behaves the way they do. There is usually a good reason for their behaviour, which can only be discovered with effective communication. You may think they are a complete fool, but you must give them the respect they deserve. You may discover that you need to go in complete opposite directions in life to them, but that is okay. They could be a homicidal maniac, suffering from depression or sexual deviance, however, these are simply labels. Whatever the behaviour, there is usually a reason for its existence.

Once you start to consider someone's reasons for their behaviour by respecting them and empathising with them, you may be surprised that they have not completely cracked under the pressure of what they have experienced. You cannot help someone by first disrespecting them, because when you do that, you are screaming that you do not understand them. It is important to suspend your own beliefs and judgements in order to authentically connect with someone.

> **The emotional response of another person, be it happy, sad or indifferent, resides on the inside of their nervous system, which is outside of your control.**

Always remember rapport

Any situation where you are feeling resistance from the other person, or they are not understanding you, suggests you have not established rapport. When you establish rapport effectively, you are instinctively more capable of discovering the needs of the person and subsequently satisfying those needs. In a sales-type situation, if your customer is resistant, it means you have not established rapport and built some common ground. In social situations, the common ground might be joining in a drink or in having a banter about your favourite sport. Essentially, you must assume that there are no resistant people, only inflexible communicators. Your ability to conduct effective communication is directly proportional to your ability to build rapport. Respecting the other person's model of the world helps build rapport; building rapport helps you understand the other person's model of the world.

> **Rapport is part of the glue that holds the fabric of society together.**

Question your understanding of the concept of right and wrong and the assumptions of the rules you choose to follow. Question whether you are blindly following rituals that are irrelevant to you today. In the same vein, challenge where you perceive your judgement of people comes from and whether this is getting in the way of respecting others' views of the world. If we eradicated the concepts of right and wrong from our view of the world, the ability to effectively communicate, build rapport and create meaningful relationships would soar.

We have all the resources we need

You are in charge of your mind and your results. You are in charge of your goals and levels of fulfilment and motivation. Your job is to operate each of these inside your own head, so you must take charge. You have all of the resources you need to achieve your desired outcomes. There is no such thing as an unresourceful person, just unresourceful emotional states. If you have seen something being done, you have the resources to be able to do that same thing. It boils down to whether you believe it or not. For example, most people know how the body looks when it is in the act of skiing. Stand up right now and act as if you are skiing down a mountain. Automatically, you will start to do what a skier does, even if you have never done it before. You already have that resource stored inside your brain in a particular area, which then allows you to access it from memory and act it out. If we shifted that resource from that part of your brain to all of the muscles and feeling associated with actually skiing, you would be able to ski!

Just to reiterate, people have all of the resources available to carry out any behaviour if they have observed it. Where it is located in your neural real estate determines whether you believe it or not. When somebody uses the word 'can't', they are lying. It might take shifting from one area to another and some practice, but fundamentally, if a thing or activity is possible for one human being, it is possible for another. As soon as you say you can't do something, it creates a block. Whether you can do the thing or not boils down to belief. If you shift that to the area of the brain which says 'I can do it,' all of a sudden, you start acting as if you can.

> **If you are broke and constantly complain about being broke, you are perpetuating being broke.**

Daniel Kish had his eyes surgically removed as a thirteen-month-old toddler due to cancer. Yet his mother brought him up as if he was a sighted person, so now he operates like a sighted person. He would walk around the house, ride his bike and do all of the things that sighted people do with ease. How did he do this? Daniel learnt the technique of echolocation. Echolocation is the ability to detect objects by sensing echoes from those objects. Daniel learned to make clicking sounds with his mouth and these sounds would bounce off objects, which would give him a sense of the object's location. Daniel has now become a world expert in echolocation, and trains blind children how to 'see'.

If you are broke and are constantly complaining about being poor, you will perpetuate being poor. A person who is wealthy did not become so by walking around with the belief of being broke. You must believe that there is gold everywhere, because there is. All you have to do is pick it up. The moment you start believing and acting as if there are opportunities for you to make money, the opportunities will present themselves because your perception has changed. People who exist in poverty have been trained to be in poverty. Poverty, sadness, depression, addiction, illness and anxiety are all a behavioural compass. Time to change your compass if you are serious about mastering the good life.

Create wholeness

Everything that we are learning here is designed to increase wholeness. If you look at computer systems, they function because of the different parts working together as a unit. The more fragmented those parts are, the slower the system; the more integrated the parts are, the faster the system. This is true for most systems. When working with people, your goal is to bring together all of the parts that increase wholeness. When dealing with a person, it is important to bring all aspects of their personality together under one leadership and reach a state of unity so there is a clarity in the direction they are moving in.

Fail forward fast for fulfilment

To every action, there is an equal and opposite reaction. There is, therefore, no such thing as failure, only results. If you do something and get a result you don't like, you change the behaviour to get a different result. If you don't like the result, you continue changing the behaviour until you get the result you desire. In life, the people that achieve are the people that persist. Generally, people don't just fall into success, they keep on failing until they succeed. It's the FFFF rule: Failing Forward Fast for Fulfilment!

I attended a convention recently and Deepak Chopra was presenting. Deepak is a world-renowned author and respected authority in personal empowerment and change. He spoke about the fact that when he first started, no one wanted to publish his book. He printed at least 1,000 copies of his book. He contacted many of the main publishers, and no one was interested. He repeated the process and sent it out again and again. He refused to give up. He got to where he is now because of persistence.

Kim McCosker, another presenter at the same convention, had a similar experience in that she could not get a publishing deal when she first started. She wrote a cookbook even though she had no professional experience in cooking or writing. She contacted every publisher she could and got turned down by every one of them. Eventually, she self-published and took herself and her books on the road. She travelled from town to town, doing signings in book shops. Her book became a best seller, and eventually, she got a publishing deal with Hay House Publishing.

When 'Colonel' Harland David Sanders retired, he realised he did not have enough money to live on. As a consequence, he decided to try to license his secret chicken recipe to various restaurants. He went from restaurant to restaurant, living in his car. He was rejected over and over again, in excess of 1,000 rejections, but every time he got rejected his skill grew. His idea for a secret chicken recipe eventually grew into what became the world-famous Kentucky Fried Chicken franchise.

The world is full of unemployed geniuses and people with potential who are broke. The one thing that drives the bus is persistence. You fail until you succeed, not the other way around.

Every time you fail, you learn something that will fast forward your success. Have your dream and keep going for it. Get in and start failing with gusto! The more you do it, the more you learn.

There is a millionaire's club in the USA which will not allow you to become a member unless you are a self-made millionaire and you have been bankrupt at least twice! In their minds, unless you have been bankrupt, you are just not playing the business game. Successful people fail more than their unsuccessful counterparts. For example, Dick Smith, the Australian entrepreneur and philanthropist, went bankrupt three times before becoming a multimillionaire.

> **Failure is just a learning process. Failure is just feedback.**

Babe Ruth was a baseball player famous for hitting more home runs in one season than any other baseball player in history. However, at one point he also held the record for the most strikeouts than any other player, a fact which is often conveniently forgotten when talking about his success. It appears on the surface that most famous people out there are overnight sensations.

This impression is supported when seemingly overnight the media latches onto someone and spreads word of their fame. However, often these celebrities worked tirelessly, continually failing for years before achieving success. The classic example of this is Willie Nelson. He was extremely disciplined and used to write a song every single day. If you look at the top forty songs over the last, say, forty years, Willie Nelson's name keeps cropping up time and time again.

What we have been indoctrinated to believe is that failure is bad and when you fail you should give up. All of these examples prove that failure is just part of the learning and succeeding process.

Pay attention to the response

The meaning of a communication is the response that you get. If a boy goes up to a pretty girl and tells her 'I love you' and she smacks him on the head, what is the meaning of the communication? The meaning 'I love you' equals 'Hit to the head'. It has nothing to do with the boy's intention, but everything to do with what came back to him. It's as simple as that. If he says 'I love you' and she kisses him, then that is what 'I love you' means to her. If he says 'I love you' and she starts taking her clothes off, then that is what 'I love you' means to her! There is no argument, no dispute.

Power lies in flexibility

The law of requisite variety states that the person with the most flexibility within a system will control the system. It doesn't matter how intelligent you are, how beautiful, how ugly, how powerful or how weak you are. None of those things matter. The person who has the most flexibility is the one who will gain control.

> **The person with the most flexibility prevails.**

Many behaviourists will tell you that humans control the planet because they have opposable thumbs and larger brains. I believe it is primarily because of our stomachs. We can pretty much eat anything. In addition, there is no specific mating season for humans! There is an interesting documentary in which a Chinese biologist, Dr Pan Wenshi, talks about the survival of the giant panda bear.

His team had done everything they could to keep the pandas alive and procreating and accepted that if the panda became extinct, it was their own fault. There were a number of reasons for this. First, it is extremely difficult to work out the sex of a panda, making it even more difficult to get them to mate. Maybe they themselves are confused about their sexuality! Second, the female is only on heat two to three days of the entire year. Third, they only eat one or two special types of bamboo plant, which are found in a very specific region. If they eat such specialist food which is only found in one place and they hardly have sex, the chances of them surviving in the wild are remote. They are a biological dead end. They are restricted in terms of where they can live because of what they eat. Human beings, on the other hand, can live anywhere from the Arctic to the most tropical regions in the world and everything in between, and we can reproduce at any time we please. When it comes to food, we can eat just about anything.

It is important to understand the power of flexibility we hold within our own minds. Each thought that we have will determine our progress or outcome. When the ground beneath you starts to open up in the middle of an earthquake, do you say to yourself: 'That shouldn't be happening, so I'm just going to stay right where I am' or, 'Time to make a run for it'? Your ability to be flexible in your thinking is about not being attached to what you knew to be true in history but being observant to what is happening in the present and behaving in accordance with this. Your survival depends on your flexibility, and so does your desired outcome.

Instead of looking at the results of our choices as either being a success or a failure, realise that it is simply a measurement of the thoughts and actions you have taken. You can then go and adjust your thoughts and actions to create a better-suited outcome, which you might call success. Either way, you have always had the power within you to create the outcome you wish. A little fine-tuning of your thoughts will bring you closer to your desired outcomes. Sometimes it is really just a matter of seeing it and then believing you can do it. By the end of this book, you will be able to work out if you are fixed in a narrow way of doing things or not. You will learn to increase the scope of your behavioural flexibility to do things outside your old scope of conditioning.

As a young boy, Peter Gray was injured in a wagon accident which resulted in an amputation of his right arm; his dominant arm. Gray's enthusiasm for baseball led him to learn to bat and field one-handed, catching the ball in his glove and then quickly removing his glove and transferring the ball to his hand in one motion. It got to a point where he could do this faster than many two-handed players. Peter became an American professional baseball outfielder who played in the Major League Baseball and was an inspiration to many people. He didn't care that most people thought you needed two arms to play baseball. He conceptualised a way to do it and he just did it. If you can't do it one way, discover another way.

One breath away

This moment could be one breath away from not making it, just one moment away from death. Every time you drive a car, you are taking a risk with your life. Many of us spend enormous amounts of time terrified of death, resulting in the pleasure of living our life being stolen. The American Indians have an interesting philosophy when it comes to death: 'Death is my shadow. I can try and outrun it or I can befriend it.' It may sound strange, but I think this is a good attitude to have. It is a gentle way of being. Once you fully embrace that any moment could be your last, you can relax and be present in living. To spend even a moment worrying about it is simply a waste of that moment. Insurance companies, banks and other institutions prey on this fear. They fertilise it with marketing and advertising campaigns. The wealthiest and the most powerful people on earth all end up the same way: in the ground.

Life comes in many colours

There is a dualistic mentality which pervades society: thinking in terms of black and white. In reality, there is a continuum of colours and this applies to everything. Religion has much to answer in this regard, because many religions espouse the belief that there is only right and wrong, which is not realistic in the context of our world. This type of indoctrination inevitably leads to individuals spending enormous amounts of time obsessing about right and wrong, trying to work out puzzles that can't be worked out.

When Einstein said everything is relative, he upset many physicists who were fixated on a dualistic way of looking at science.

When I observe gender, I see a continuum. Some people have strong male characteristics and some have strong female characteristics and some have something in between. Using either a vagina or a penis and set of testicles to classify gender is using the black-and-white classification method. Today, there is far more freedom in sexuality. Do what makes you happy and do what gives you meaning. Expressing your freedom to be who you are is living a meaningful life.

> **Life is full of disappointments and pleasant surprises. We should learn from and make the most of both. —Colin Ball**

Contemplation and affirmation

A number of my students and clients have asked me to clarify the process of contemplation and how it differs or is similar to the process of affirmation.

Our mind operates in at least two distinct realms. The first realm is the one of creating new neural pathways in our brain. In parallel, new behaviours are generated. The act of contemplation follows this first realm. The second realm is entering into the world of metaphysics and quantum physics. This is the world of expressing intention through vibration, frequency and harmonics. The process of affirmation operates in this realm.

Royalty, presidents, billionaires, inventors and entertainers have all used affirmation to create abundance and, in some cases, influence and power. The realm of quantum physics has its origins in pre-Egyptian time. Religious systems of the world and esoteric communities including the Masons, the Knights Templar and the Illuminati have all harnessed the power of quantum physics. In more recent history the book and movie, *The Secret*, has packaged up quantum physics neatly into a concept they called The Law of Attraction.

The process of contemplation

The process of contemplation is a string of questions with the central aim of discovering how to arrive at an outcome.

Let's start off with the statement, 'I am a love magnet'. What does this mean? It might mean attracting more friends. By following this question-answer format, we have created a link between the statement, 'I am a love magnet' and the concept of having more friends. Once this realisation is made, we start again with the statement, 'I am a love magnet', and this time we might zoom in on what attitude leads to attracting love. By continuing the stream of questions, you create a new neural association that arrives at one or more possible answers. The primary purpose of contemplation is that every time we create new associations it has an effect on what we see in the world of physical reality. This in turn expands our awareness. We begin to see things that were always there, but we were perceptually blind to them before.

Here are some questions typically used to elicit the contemplation process.

- What does this mean?
- Why is this important to me?
- What are the positives of this?
- What are the negatives of this?
- Am I worthy of this?
- What would step one be?
- And the next step? And the next?
- Who can help me with this?
- Who else is involved in this?
- How are they involved?
- What will it feel like to have/be/do this?

Employing the process of contemplation before the affirmation process is strongly recommended because it clarifies the finer details of the goal/event/outcome that you desire. Contemplation also uncovers any internal conflict or resistance that may inhibit you from reaching your desired end. Any internal resistance or conflict must be resolved first before you enter the affirmation process. When the affirmation process fails, the primary reason is usually because some part of you is not aligned with the desired end point, regardless of the level of conscious investment in it. This is why contemplation is just as important as affirmation when it comes to manifesting your desired outcome.

The process of affirmation

1. Decide on a goal, event or outcome you desire. Use the contemplation process to fine-tune your desired outcome.
2. In your mind, hold the image of you having completed that goal/event/outcome.
3. Continue to hold that image whilst you experience all of the feelings and sensations of having reached the completion point. Suspend reality and take on the state of actually having reached the outcome. Activate your senses: see it; hear it; feel it.
4. Repeat Steps 2 and 3 each morning on rising and each night before going to sleep.

Note: If you are affirming a large long-term goal, then break it down into mini-goals and complete the affirmation process for each one in turn. Lastly, complete the affirmation process for the end target goal.

How does the process of affirmation work? The emotion you experience vibrates at a particular frequency and harmonises with things in the environment of the same frequency. To explain this in simplistic terms, like energy attracts like energy. If I'm vibrating joy then I attract others who are also joyful. The most powerful transformation begins with love and compassion vibrating from your heart.

PART IV

Relationships Revolution

WELCOME TO THE MOST important part of the book, where I'll be sharing with you what I've learnt from studying relationships over a thirty-year period. The quality of our relationships determines the level of fulfilment in our lives. We feel most whole when we feel we belong. Mastering the good life is about forming deeper connections with others and feeling valued. What I have observed in my clients and students who find their 'tribe' is that their self-esteem improves, their sense of purpose increases and their overall wellbeing is enhanced. In this part of the book you'll learn advanced communication tools to advance your personal, intimate and business relationships. Finally, I'll be guiding you in a method of harmonising and creating authentic relationships called The Seven Hearts. In completing this part, you'll arrive at a deeper loving connection with the most important person in your world: you.

> **Never take an action against another that in the long term would harm yourself.**

CHAPTER 14

RELATIONSHIPS ARE LIFE

Life is relationships in motion

In nature, animals, plants, bacteria and other microbes have a commensal relationship with each other in order for life to sustain. It is truly a beautiful phenomenon.

Meanwhile, many relationships in nature are symbiotic. It's a give-and-take dynamic, an exchange of resources for the mutual benefit of each player. The remora fish, also known as the sucker fish, spends its life on and around a shark or other large sea animal. The remora cleans loose flakes of skin and faeces from its host and in return is protected from other larger predators. Mmm, it's a nice thing humans aren't that into eating each other's faeces.

It may sound like I'm talking Biology 101 here. Well, you're spot on. Not only because we are governed largely by our biology, but also because the metaphor of how organisms survive and thrive is perfect for understanding our relationships with others, with ourselves and our community.

Human relationships can be prey-predator or mutually beneficial. Ultimately, to survive and thrive boils down to the laws of nature, which are all about the dynamic and the balance of resources. If you struggle to understand how world wars and global political oppression occurs, look closer to home and you will discover the same patterns playing out in your close social circle, in your own backyard.

There is a huge disconnect between humanity and Mother Earth; there has been a relationship breakdown. This is because we have become disconnected from ourselves and with each other. The cure for the pandemic of dis-ease is not about killing a mysterious invader. That would be the equivalent of repairing your broken front door lock when the roof has already caved in. The solution is to reconnect humanity with Mother Earth. The pollution in our air and water has reached pandemic proportions. The chemicals in our soil and all through our food chain is causing diabolical weakness in our immune systems. Our immune system is billions of years old and is designed to protect us, but over the past two hundred years has become compromised by manmade toxic environmental invaders. First fix your house, your environment. I presented a concept called easy-hard, hard-easy in Part I. This concept is so relevant to our relationship with nature. First do the hard part: clean up and boost the vitality of our earth first, then the easy part follows – your health, vitality and longevity.

Can you experience life with some level of control and direction or are you at the mercy of Mother Earth and the social and political structures placed around us? I believe we have control over the many moving parts of our lives. We have a huge array of choices and abilities to influence the level of satisfaction and enjoyment we can experience in life. We have the opportunity to learn new skills; we have the opportunity to change our responses to events; we have options of how we feel, and how we perceive the meaning of our existence when we are flowing along the river of life. We have an option to be flexible and adapt to what is occurring on the outside of us. We can make a choice and one which is not bound by any expectation.

Mastering the good life is about connecting with your true nature – communicating authentically with yourself and others. I'm talking about all levels of verbal and non-verbal communication. And communication is two-way traffic. It's being understood and also understanding another.

What do you think it would feel like if every time you had a conversation with someone, there was a resounding clarity and calmness? Imagine if every time you spoke to someone about a problem, you were deeply understood. Often our problems won't shift because we are not being understood, we are not being heard. Often our problems exist because we are not connecting with our real feelings and we are not collaborating with others through mutual respect and with effective communication skills.

Imagine the implications in your workplace – so many possibilities. Understanding your client's needs, connecting with your team, being understood by your manager. Your job would be far more satisfying, enjoyable and successful.

For me, this is a beautiful place to be. The joy that I have when teaching this subject is immense. Every person I reach becomes a member of this happy, relaxed, adventurous club that goes out there and creates. People who truly enjoy living. One writer put it most eloquently by saying, 'The whole point of personal development of this nature is to become unreasonably happy.' No, not just reasonably happy, UNREASONABLY HAPPY! This implies that no matter what is going on around you, you are happy for the sake of being happy. If you could pass that gift on to others, what would occur? If you could take a good dose of it yourself, what would happen? I suggest that you give it to yourself first, then you can give it away with grace.

Connection and belonging

As an animal, there is safety in being part of a group. For humans, beyond the question of safety and survival, being a member of a tribe or a community gives you security and support to explore and expand more than if you were doing it alone. Belonging is a powerful unconscious program that is built into our biology. Some of us are misfits in our community and others thrive with strong social networks. Feeling more connected to others where you easily establish meaningful relationships is about having great skills in the area of communication and rapport.

Being lonely is a symptom of being disconnected. Loneliness has become a common experience in our society today. I'm not referring to being alone, since loneliness is often experienced within marriages, within an expansive friend network and even within part of a large family. Many individuals are lonely within such long-term relationships because the connection has been lost or maybe it was never present.

Before we launch into the details of how to improve your connections through communication mastery, I have a quick and powerful tip to share with you. It is much more powerful for someone to arrive at an answer from within themselves than to be given or told the answer. Rather than you telling the other person something, they 'tell' themselves. Presenting questions to invite a person to the area of a particular answer is an art form. For a person to offer their answer, it is more respectful, and their answers are aligned with their beliefs and values.

Telling a person: You are the type of person who likes to dance and not run for exercise.

Leading with a question: I am wondering is it true you like to dance and not run for exercise?

Curiously observant

One of the fundamentals of good communication is being observant. How do you become observant? Become curious first. This is your motivation to start watching and paying attention to the person you are interacting with. Every utterance they make is important, and so too is everything they don't say. People are constantly leaking information about what they think, value and believe. Anyone can learn the art of observation with practice, time and curiosity.

I know what you mean

How often do you experience common misunderstandings associated with the use of language when conversing with others? When I say a word, any word, you have to realise that the word is only a representation of the thing I am describing, not the actual thing. If I were to say the word 'love' to you, you would automatically imagine what I am talking about. Your interpretation of the word might be similar to mine due to common experience, but it is unlikely that it would have the same attributes and feelings associated with it. The thing that I describe is therefore only what I think it is. What I think exists in my mind as a set of complex associations. In other words, every time I have experienced love, talked about love, seen a movie about love or observed others in love, a new file was added to the love folder in my mind. Your mind, your files and your folders are unique to you. From now on, when someone says, 'I know what you mean,' you will automatically translate it as follows, 'I know what that means to me on the inside of *my* head.' Take the time to appreciate the associations and meanings that others may have so each of you can be heard and understood.

When one person reads a religious text like the Bible, they may see nothing but love, yet when another person reads the very same text, they may see nothing but vengeance and retribution.

Rapport: The art of connection

Have you ever met someone and instantly liked them? Have you had the feeling that you've known them for years? Have you had the experience of finishing another person's sentences? Or knowing what they're about to say before they say it? How about a warm fuzzy feeling in the pit of your stomach the moment you meet someone? If you've ever had any of these experiences you've experienced a good rapport. Imagine if you could establish this with everyone you meet! What would happen to your social life? What would happen to your sales figures, knowing that people buy more from people they like? What would happen to your prospects of promotion if you could do this with your managers? How would your intimate relationships improve?

Rapport is the unconscious recognition of similarity. This is when you meet someone and are drawn to them because the other person seems like you. As humans, we naturally like things that are like us. Similarly, we recoil or step away from things which are not like us.

> **Racism only exists because people point out the differences between groups. The moment you start to focus on the similarities, you break this down.**

Fighting between religions only occurs because of others pointing out the differences. The moment people start to focus on similarities, the necessity for violence and atrocity in the name of religion falls away.

Human beings naturally communicate through body language, tone of voice and words. It may surprise you to learn that fifty-five per cent of communication occurs through body language. Thirty-eight per cent of communication happens via tone of voice and the remainder, a mere seven per cent of communication, happens via the content, the words themselves. Most people mistakenly concentrate on the content when they're communicating and are not aware of the messages their body and tone of voice are sending. Similarly, babies, who can't yet speak, learn and express themselves through body language and tone of voice.

The most sensible thing to do is to invest more time and energy improving and understanding body language and tonal qualities. Unfortunately, body language is often the least taught mode of communication in our childhood years, especially in the education system.

The power of rapport

Many communication trainers teach rapport as if its core purpose is to make everyone like you. Let's get something straight here: rapport is not about being *liked*, rapport is about being *like*, being *similar*. If someone is angry at you, be angry back, but instead of using words to inflame the situation, choose respectful words but match tonal quality and intensity of emotion. This will calm the situation down, as it diffuses the emotion. Imagine the following scenario: someone shouts at you, 'What the hell are you doing, staring at my wife?' You yell back, 'You are absolutely right, I was admiring your wife's shoes!' They would be expecting a fight, but what can they say to a response like that? There is nothing to say.

But you would have been heard. You created rapport because you matched intensity and tone of voice. There is an awful lot of fun you can have with this subject. The more you learn, the more you can do and play with it and the more creative and natural you become. Being able to suspend your own style of communication to make connections is key.

Rapport elements

In this section, I'm going to take you through the detailed technical areas of rapport, encompassing: keywords, senses cues, content chunks, common experiences and body language.

Keywords

People often repeat the same words or phrases over and over when they talk. Examples include 'Okay', 'You know what I mean?', 'Like' and 'Yeah'. Different cultures have their own keywords, which have filtered into the language. In Beijing, for example, people insert a 'nah' sound at the end of every sentence. To enhance rapport with others, listen out for keywords in conversations with others and include those keywords in your communication with them, which will lead to an unconscious recognition of similarity.

Sense cues

How a person interfaces with the outside world can be categorised into six sense areas: visual (seeing), kinaesthetic (feeling), auditory (hearing), olfactory (smelling), gustatory (tasting) and internal dialogue (thinking). All people use all six areas to varying degrees; however, most people have a favoured sense area. Learning the cues of each of the sense areas is a matter of learning the types of words to watch for. In the context of rapport, observe what the other person's favoured sense area is and match it by using words from the same sense area in your sentences back to them.

Visual word cues describe the qualities of an image such as colourful, bright, shiny, glowing, reflection, location, near, far, moving, still, flat, 3D, small, large. The statement 'I *see* what you mean' is a big hint that they are operating from the visual part of the brain.

Kinaesthetic word cues describe sensations such as rough, heavy, light, slow, fast, hot, cold, vibration, sinking. The statement 'I *feel* what that is like' is an indicator that they are operating from the kinaesthetic part of their brain.

Auditory word cues describe sound qualities such as loud, soft, sharp, high pitched, low pitched, sporadic, steady. 'I *hear* that you're an expert at that' is an indicator they are operating from the auditory part of their brain.

Olfactory word cues describe smelling qualities such as musty, sweet, delicious, rancid. 'I smelt fear in the air'.

Gustatory word cues describe taste qualities such as sweet, salty, bitter, sour. 'I could taste the success'.

Olfactory and gustatory word cues have a significant overlap, as the nose and the mouth are anatomically connected and often what you smell is what you taste and vice versa.

Internal dialogue word cues describe thinking qualities such as discussion, calculation, assessment, judgement, weighing up pros and cons. 'Adding up the pros and the cons led me to this conclusion'.

Content chunks

People deal with different quantities of information in different ways, and often you can detect this in a simple greeting.

Peta returns home from work and is greeted by her flatmate, Ann.

'How was your day today?' she asks.

'Fine,' Peta replies.

Ann looks at Peta expectantly, waiting for her to share further information, but she doesn't have any more information she finds worth sharing.

'How was your day?' Peta asks.

Ann proceeds to go into great detail about every aspect of her day from going on her morning run to the way the cashier looked at her in the local supermarket.

Some people, like Peta in this example, may deem such detail unnecessary and annoying. They tend to switch off or glaze over when they feel bombarded with what they deem to be too much information. Meanwhile, Ann is someone who prefers to deal with large content chunks. She feels neglected if she isn't given lots of information and if she can't express lots of information in response. She likes to be listened to.

Pay attention to content chunks when communicating with people and match their content chunks in your conversation with them to establish rapport. This concept extends to the content chunks you choose to include in letters, emails, text messages and social media posts. If someone writes only a few lines in an email to you, then your response email should also contain only a few lines to maintain rapport.

Commonality of experience

Talking about common experiences is another way to encourage rapport. When you've just met someone for the first time, notice how quickly you become connected when you have a topic that interests both of you. It could be the commonality of having children, the cute dogs you both have, your interest in hot rod cars, your type of job or your common gripes about the cost of living.

Body language

The most powerful rapport method is in reading and expressing the unspoken language: body language. As a reminder of the statistic I mentioned above, a whopping fifty-five per cent of communication occurs through the physiology of the body. What I'm referring to here is body positions and angles, movements and the level of muscle tension.

In my classes, I sit in front of the group and move my hand up and down slowly, just a few inches and in time with my breathing, which is my unconscious connection to the group. Then I gradually slow the movement of my hand and the breathing rate of the room in turn slows down and the group goes into a peaceful, relaxed trance. I have used this technique effectively on a group of nearly a thousand doctors.

When onstage entertainers get everyone to stand up and wave side to side, they are establishing leadership and rapport with the audience. Human beings really are that attracted to similarity and connection.

Mothers demonstrate rapport with their babies all the time. When the mother is upset, the baby is upset and vice versa. That's how it works with babies, because they communicate only through their body language.

Allison was invited for a night out with a close friend. I received a call from her informing me her friend was going to have to leave the event and return home early as her partner was having difficulties with their newborn baby, who wouldn't stop crying.

Allison asked if I could help, so I called the new dad. I guided him to hold his young daughter and every time she took a breath in preparing to let out a cry, I advised him to ever so lightly squeeze her around her ribs. As she exhaled with a cry, I had him gently release the squeeze. In no time at all she was asleep in his arms and Allison and her friend continued with their night out!

Below I'll be explaining the three steps in body language rapport.

Step 1: Body language: Matching and mirroring body positions

The first step is to mirror or match the other person's body position or angle. To mirror someone is to literally copy what they are doing as if you were looking into a mirror. Matching someone is when you match what they do. If they lean on their right fist, you lean on your right fist. If they cross their right leg, you cross your right leg. A subtle mirroring of body language is turning your right foot out to mirror someone's right turned-out leg.

Step 2: Body language: Pacing body movement

Pacing is where you copy the pace at which the other person is moving while you are communicating. For example, if you and I were having a conversation right now and you were gesticulating with your hands, rather than be really obvious with my movement I would choose to move just my fingers. The key is to move them at the same time as your hand movement.

Step 3: Body language: Leading body movement

Continuing on from pacing, if I were to suddenly change what I was doing, for example, start using the other hand and you followed me, instantly I would know that we had established rapport because I have led the new gesture.

How far can you push the rapport?

You may be concerned, understandably, that intentionally and artificially creating rapport could come across as you being fake. This is where the subject of congruency comes in, because if you are congruent you can be as overt as you want when building rapport with people. Let me give you a real-life example of what I mean by being overt but being congruent. I was once talking with someone I'd met in the street who had the ability to lift his eyebrow when he was talking. I don't have this ability, as I'm simply not wired that way. Instead of struggling to copy him, I literally used my finger to subtly lift my eyebrow every time he did it. Instantly, the conversation became more fluid, friendly and open. It worked perfectly!

Practising rapport

While I was learning rapport, I practised rapport exercises on a regular twenty-minute train journey. On one occasion, I established rapport with a guy. By the end of the journey, I knew he was a divorcé, was newly married, was trying for a baby with his new wife, and he had a low sperm count! The essential takeaway here is respect.

I recall a time when my rapport skills helped me to track down a guy who had run into the back of my car on the Sydney Harbour Bridge in the middle of peak-hour traffic on Christmas Eve ... just a minor nightmare. At the time of the accident, we exchanged phone numbers and he gave me his address. I then tried for months to get through to this guy by phoning and texting him, but he was neither picking up the phone nor returning my calls.

Eventually, Allison and I decided to make a hundred-kilometre journey to his house. When we arrived, we discovered he had moved out of that address three weeks before. In establishing rapport with the new occupant by matching her body position and muscle tension, we were given the information that he had previously rented through a real estate agent situated a few kilometres away in the town centre. So, off we went to visit this real estate agent. There, I established rapport with the front desk clerk by mirroring her head angle, and she gave me his new address. (If you understand the law around privacy and security, you'll understand this was quite a feat.) We drove on to the guy at his new address, where he told me he had intended to call me back. Mmm, likely story. Needless to say, we secured his insurer's details at that point. The good news ending is that the insurer fixed our car.

I have many other stories just like this one where my rapport skills opened many closed doors for me. Many individuals naturally have advanced rapport skills with zero training – they learnt how to establish rapport during childhood, likely through modelling their parents and caregivers. What I am teaching you here will fill in any missing gaps in learning, so you have the same opportunities as rapport experts.

How much rapport?

The amount or level of rapport that you build depends on your objective. In business, you want to have a degree of understanding and you need to identify with one another. If you're in an intimate relationship, you'll be establishing deep rapport. A deep level of rapport has been established when one person starts a sentence, and another person finishes. When you are in sync with another at the level of their thoughts, you know you're in deep rapport!

CHAPTER 15

RELATIONSHIP MAGIC

Three of me

Most relationships follow the pattern of a dynamic relationship cycle (DRC) where there are three roles being played out: victim, bully and saviour. Each player will have a strong affinity with one of the roles, the one that is most comfortable or familiar. What role someone is playing may not be immediately obvious. In the 1960s, psychologist Dr Stephen Karpman coined the term 'drama triangle' to describe this interplay. I have given it a new name in this book because I don't necessarily see this interplay as always akin to a drama. That said, understanding DRC is useful for gaining insights into dysfunctional or challenging relationships that are often dramatic and intense.

The three roles

The three roles in the DRC are dependent on each other. You can't have any of them without at least one of the others being in place. Although most people favour one of the three roles, ultimately, we can play any of the three roles depending on the context of the relationship, environment or circumstance.

Victim (prey, the wounded, target)
This is the 'poor me' person who has come to feel helpless and passive and looks for a rescuer to justify these feelings. Their victim status is held in place by either a real or perceived persecutory person, or oppressive situation. The victim sees themselves as not being responsible for the disempowered situation they find themselves in. They feel powerless to the happenings around them.

Bully (persecutor, predator, protester, pursuer)
The person who bullies, blames, criticises and oppresses victims: 'It's all your fault (pointing finger at the victim)'. The bully can be a predator that attempts to use power and control to manipulate the extraction of resources from the prey.

Saviour (rescuer, helper, liberator, crusader, warrior, protector, defender)
The 'let me help you' person whose own guilt often drives them to compulsive and chronic rescuing of victims. Charities are rescuers, as are counsellors, health practitioners, fire-fighters and any person in the 'helping' profession.

All relationships, societies and countries operate largely through a DRC structure. Understanding how this system works and how to become an observer of the three roles in this cycle will give you immense insight into your inner and outer world.

Imagine a family situation where the mother chastises her child for not making the swimming team. The child runs crying to the father, complaining about the mother. The father challenges the mother for chastising the child. In this situation, the mother is the bully, the child is the victim and the father is the saviour.

The interesting thing about this DRC is that the roles can change quickly. Think of the different roles as wearing different hats. The people in the DRC wear different hats depending on the situation. This cycle can be seen in all walks of life. It can be seen in corporate structures, family structures, social structures, media, government structures and even between countries. A fun exercise to do is to watch any online streamed drama show or movie and observe who is playing which part. You can do this same exercise with your intimate relationships, your workplace, your friend circle, your family unit. Particularly observe yourself and what hat you wear and in which context and in relation to which people.

I believe it is healthy to play out a DRC in society with one condition, that you don't get bound to one of the roles. To be bound to one role can prove tiresome and this is also where problems pervade. People can become confused between their character and the interchangeable hats they wear. They can become identified with the role. It's not healthy to keep seeking out DRC as a pastime, or for it to become an addiction. By limiting yourself to one of the DRC roles it's likely you will have an inappropriate response to a particular situation. All wars and battles include victims, bullies (the invader or attacker), and saviours (allies).

Solution 1: Transforming each role

Transforming each of the roles so that they are additive rather than deductive is key. The new roles have core aims of creation, support and self-empowerment.

The victim transforms their expression into a creator. As a creator you discover new ways of behaving and finding solutions. You acquire help from a guide or coach when needed and you are ready to put your skin in the game whereas before you perpetually leant on others without expending any of your own energy and resources and stayed stuck in a hole.

The bully transforms their expression into a challenger. The challenger gives constructive feedback and advice. The challenger is a point of friction for the creator so that the creator is able to respond in growth rather than retract in fear and resentment. A bully may fail to maintain a respectful challenger role if they encounter an individual that victimises themselves and chooses to remain in that limiting role.

The saviour transforms their expression into a guide. The professionals that guide include coaches, therapists and NLP practitioners. A guide can also be a friend that has overcome a similar obstacle to whatever the challenged individual is facing. A guide does not jump into the hole with the person being challenged. A guide understands where their support boundaries are, and they understand they aren't responsible for someone else's choice to remain victimised. A guide may revert back into being a saviour if they are interfacing with a victim who chooses not to become a creator of their life. When facing a rigid victim mentality, the guide may best be of service to themselves and the victim by stepping away.

In the transformed state, each role perpetuates the new and positively affirming DRC. A creator is supported by being guided and challenged rather than being persecuted and rescued. A challenger is not triggered into being a bully as the victim no longer exists. A guide is relieved of their duties of being responsible for a victim and simply offers guidance.

Solution 2: Becoming an observer

When the going gets tough in a relationship, step out of the cycle and observe. Then decide on a plan of action. A great example of this comes from my own life. It was 2010 and my partner Allison and I had just moved the business to a new commercial location in Sydney, Australia. It was a sizeable investment for 180 square meters of commercial space. Within a few days of moving in, we received a letter from the electricity company stating they were going to begin extensive construction works across the road from our office for the next eight months. Of course, they apologised for the inconvenience. This was bad news for us. It meant we were not going to be able to conduct our business from our new location, as jackhammers and hypnosis classes don't mix well! Allison and I put our heads together from a detached perspective, with no emotion whatsoever. We decided the best course of action would be to exploit the DRC relationship. I called a face-to-face meeting with the electricity company's project managers. They agreed to meet, and two of them arrived at our offices.

I began by asking them to recognise that the consequence of their construction project was that I would be paying office rent, but not have the use of my office. I, therefore, would not be able to earn any money for the next eight months while they did the development work.

'Yes,' came the reply. 'We do apologise for any inconvenience caused.'

Allison then began to cry and acted upset (her behaviour was authentic).

'Okay,' I said calmly, 'well, that means that I will have nothing better to do over the next eight months than to spend all my time rallying all the businesses that you will negatively affect to completely f**k up your entire construction plan. If you drop one piece of paper on the street, I will be there. If you have a machine running a minute over-time, I will be there. I will do whatever it takes to share with you the pain and discomfort that you have given to us. You should know that I am a master hypnotist, so it will be easy to rally the people required to make this project both expensive and hellish for you.'

The two individuals looked at each other in shock and then quietly made their departure. Within the hour we received a call from them to see if we could come to an arrangement. The outcome was that they covered the cost of an alternative venue for us to operate from while they completed the building work. Over time we discovered that they had lied in the first place, as the project took eighteen months and not eight to complete.

If Allison and I had both just played the victim, it would have led us nowhere. But with me taking on the unexpected role of bully, together we forced them into the role of saviour.

The point is that in any potential DRC situation, it is vital to observe the situation from a neutral position and then decide on the most appropriate hat to wear. In this particular situation, it was clear that the role I chose to take forced the company to think about the potential consequences of me rallying a group of annoyed neighbours against them. Losing even one day of building on-site could lead to a loss of significantly more dollars than they would lose by keeping us happy. This company would not have paid up unless they absolutely had to. We realised that the factors involved in their decision-making would be entirely economic, so we pushed the right buttons and got the best outcome for the situation. We were able to do this because we took on the neutral, emotionally detached position of observer *first*, before making a decision on how to act and what hat to wear in the dynamic relationship cycle.

If we had not developed the behavioural flexibility to wear each hat in the DRC, the outcome could have been very different. That's the whole point of the DRC. You are more than just one role that you play in your life. The formation of which hat you are going to wear predominately is developed in early childhood. If Mum, Dad, or a big brother or sister constantly run to your aid the moment it looks as if you have hurt yourself, you will develop a victim trait. This teaches us if we demonstrate need, someone will come and help us. If you as a young child are positively praised for coming to the aid of another or being generous, this is how you develop the helper or rescuer trait. Meanwhile, the development of the persecutor is equally straightforward. This occurs when you're praised and rewarded for your manipulation and win-at-all-cost competitive traits. Individuals who bully others often have been bullied in history.

As the observer, you become aware of the fact that there are multiple possible answers. The decision that is right for you will be dependent on the direction in which you are headed and the outcomes you desire. Conflict occurs when you come into contact with someone in a situation with a different objective to yours. How well you both navigate the conflict will be dependent on how respectful you are to each other's map of the world and how much rapport you establish between you.

When you look at the DRC as an observer, you start to realise that every answer is correct from a certain point of view. This doesn't mean that you will never come into conflict with anyone ever again. However, as an observer you have the vantage point of understanding why the conflict takes place. It occurs because you have a different purpose and path to the other party or parties involved. You can then make a conscious decision to take a different path rather than waste energy arguing. The end result is you will find yourself surrounded with people who are going in the same direction, which brings us back to the subject of values and living in flow with nature.

As you scale up to an organisation and a country level, you will begin to realise that fear is the emotion that is used to drive DRC reactions from people. An effective way to control populations is by creating a division such as white vs black or straight vs gay or mandatory vaccination vs body rights, and then stand back and watch the DRC unfold. Understanding the game and playing within it is what will help you to progress on your journey. The moment you step back and observe, you become free of the game. The moment you step back from your child begging you for more money to buy drugs, you have released yourself from the role of saviour and closed off the perpetuating victimisation of your child.

Your next practical task is to practise stepping out of the game and observing how the DRC plays out in your life. Experiment with your level of flexibility in wearing different hats. If you observe yourself perpetually in one role and you're being drawn away from your desired path, this is the perfect opportunity for you to introspect and contemplate. How can you get your needs met in a healthy, balanced way without identifying as a victim, bully or saviour?

Rich relationships

Can't live with them, can't live without them. This pretty much sums up the relationship problems that walk into my clinic rooms every week.

Relationships are without a doubt the number one issue I work on within a clinical environment. Simply, because everything operates within the context of a relationship. People are in relationships with others, relationships with food, relationships with drugs, relationships with objects, relationships with careers, relationships with money, relationships with family. There is, of course, one relationship that is the foundation of all these different relationships: the relationship an individual has with themself.

Intimate relationships or close personal partnerships have the ability to produce the ultimate joy, and the loss of this joy can be devastating. Even just the fear of losing a wonderful relationship can create anxiety. You might be asking how does Robb Whitewood qualify as a relationship guide? It's a good question and one that needs to be answered before you take any further advice from me on this most important subject of all.

Simply put, I am the guy who has stuffed up more relationships than Sheldon and Sherlock combined. This might not sound like a good starting point, but without all of this experience, I would never have embarked on a discovery of methods to solve relationship issues. Each mistake, each disaster, each euphoria, each heart-crushing moment was a lesson and ignited my motivation to find understanding. I am happy to announce the last twelve years of my life have been exceptional as far as relationships are concerned. Not perfect, because relationships never are. Nevertheless, it is truly wonderful to have learnt enough to find myself in the best partnership of my life.

When people come to see me about the breakdown of a relationship (marriage, partnership, friendship, family), I am quick to point out that there are only four reasons people have issues with one another. They are: aligned values, strategies, anchors, and mismatched criteria. I'll be covering the first three reasons below. The mismatched relationship criteria element has its own comprehensive section in the following chapter, as I have dedicated twenty-five years on developing a method called The Seven Hearts.

Aligned values

Values are the cornerstone of any meaningful, loving and productive relationship. Aligned values are synonymous with being compatible. When values are not aligned, it is guaranteed there will be ongoing conflict about what activities you do together and which direction you'll travel in.

So, what are values? Values are what we deem to be highly important. This is what we have learnt to focus our attention on. Values are generally programmed into us from our earliest years. Values are established as we watch our parents go about their daily activities. We see what they do and what is important to them. Values are a person's internal compass; it tells us how we are going to spend our time, energy and resources. By the way, it is not necessary for two people who are in a partnership or friendship to have the exact same values; they do however need to be aligned with each other for any level of compatibility and harmony.

After listening to a couple speak about the issues they were having and how upsetting it all was, it was clear that Wendy loved Harry.

I gently asked Wendy, 'What are the most important things in life?'

She replied, 'Relationships, love – you know, being loved and in love – family, fun and feeling safe and secure'.

As I looked over to Harry, he seemed to be looking into space and not really paying that much attention. I stupidly asked him the same question. 'What are the most important things in life?'

Just as stupidly he replied: 'My horse. I love my horse, he is my best friend. Also, my desert racer. State qualifiers start next month.'

My attempts to interrupt him were not working, as he seemed to be totally engrossed in telling me these things, and why not?

These were his values, things that had total meaning to him. By the time Harry was describing the gooseneck trailer that transported both the horse and the desert racer, my attempts to distract him had yet again failed. The look of panic in my eyes did nothing to help the situation. Harry was so happy describing the details of the horse, the race car and the trailer.

It was at this point I noticed the expression change on Wendy's face. I thought to myself, 'Oh no, she has just figured it out.'

As we ended the session, it was encouraging to see that both parties left feeling calmer and happier. However, it was clear they were calm for completely different reasons. About three weeks later I received a call from Harry.

'She's gone! Just up and left. I just don't understand why. Everything seemed to be getting better. We haven't argued since we saw you weeks ago'. He seemed so surprised.

What I want you to understand is that neither of the value sets was correct, they were just directions. On the surface, Wendy's and Harry's situation looked painful and a disaster but it was really a success story. You see, Wendy was now free to find a partner that had similar values to her. For Harry, it was also a great win: he got to spend more time with his horse.

Friendships and family relationships and every other type of relationship combination will operate harmoniously in the large part if the values of the pair or group are in alignment. As a reminder, alignment does not mean that all values from all parties need to be exactly the same. It means that there is a strong similarity between them. Below I've presented various hypothetical value sets to describe the concept of values alignment.

Values that are aligned

Example 1: Beth's and John's top three values
Beth: My dog, trekking, learning
John: Reading, outdoors, study

Example 2: Joe's and Sam's top three values
Joe: Work, sex, gym
Sam: Health and fitness, wealth, sex

Values that are misaligned

Example 3: Paul's and Eva's top three values
Paul: Hanging with mates, watching sports on TV, horse riding
Eva: Love, painting, cuddling up and watching movies

Example 4: Liz's and Kath's top three values
Liz: Partying, fashion, holidays
Kath: Learning, meditating, self-sustainability

What type of relationship do the above pairs have, do you think? Are they lovers, spouses, friends, family, or in business? This is the subject of relationship-matching criteria that we will be looking at in depth within the next section, titled The Seven Hearts. As a hint, if Beth's top relationship criteria for a spouse is the person considering her dog as the most important thing in their life, it is unlikely Beth would marry John, or if she did, there would be a guarantee of conflict and incompatibility. Beth may like to have her dog sleep on the bed. Beth may want to have her dog attend all the activities she does. Beth is likely to spend significant household funds on the needs of her dog, such as a carer for the dog whilst she is at work. You get the picture.

How to discover someone's values has been covered in previous sections. I've included this below here too for a convenient revision.

Values Elicitation
Ask these four questions of yourself and of the other person.

1. What is the most important thing to you in life?
2. What is the next most important thing to you in life?
3. And the next?
4. And the next?

You can elicit as many values as you would like; four is usually adequate.

Alignment of values is one of the main predictors of relationship quality. When a relationship breaks down, one or both party's values may have changed since the bond was formed.

Strategies

Don't get too excited, I am not referring to a war strategy with your partners, friends or families.

Strategies are a series of unconscious steps that we go through in our minds to be able to say yes and get a great feeling. If you take the care and time to learn and ignite the strategies of another, the result is you have a fulfilled person in front of you. This has tremendous business applications for achieving sales and agreement. In the area of loving and caring relationships, learning and igniting each other's strategies will enrich the connection and grow a longer lasting bond. Many of us naturally ignite each other's strategies without consciously being aware of it. There are no special skills required to learn someone else's strategy. All that is required is a fine-tuning of your observation skills, your time and a motivated interest.

A couple came to see me for help with an issue in the bedroom. Gary was a gentle and respectful soul who wanted nothing but happiness for his partner, Sally. Here's how their strategy played out. Gary would come up to Sally and start hugging and kissing her. So far, the strategy is working well (Step A completed). Gary then noticed that there was little to no perceivable reaction to his advances (cannot proceed to Step B, strategy halted). Being a sensitive individual, he took this as Sally not being that interested, and Gary would instantly back down and walk away or roll over. Meaning in his mind, no Step B is being reached which meant no Step C and definitely no Step D. Now, when I talked to Sally to discover her strategy, I uncovered some interesting things and an explanation for both of them. Sally explained that Gary would make an advance towards her and she would love it. Gary would hold her, she would love it, kissing her passionately, oh God she was in heaven, but being a good Catholic girl, she would just stand or lie there. This failed to fulfil Gary's second step (Step B), so Gary would, of course, stop. Sally, on the other hand, was going slowly demented with sexual frustration. The solution was simple. At the point in which Sally was in the mood and heading for Step B, we installed the ability for her to take hold of a certain part of his anatomy. This, of course, fulfilled Gary's Step B, which of course led to Step C, followed by Step D, D, D.

Strategies are everywhere and in everything we do. If you take the time to discover a few of your partner's or friend's strategies and implement them, I promise a dramatic change in the quality of the relationship. Often, we could call the subject of strategies just paying close attention. How do they drink their tea – with or without sugar? What gesture or facial expression means it is wine time? How do they feel valued and cared for?

Do you know of friendships or families where fighting and anger is a crucial part of each of their strategies? Igniting each other's strategies does not always equal calm.

How about you discover a couple of your friend's *fun* strategies. Does your friend find fun in going on a holiday that involves surf, sun, partying? Or does your friend enjoy working in the vegetable patch and sharing cups of organic tea and homemade cake? Discovering what your friend's fun strategy is to observe and ask your friend questions on what fun means to them and figure out the steps in order to achieve that fun. The order of the steps is as important as the steps themselves.

If you have a partner, you could observe your partner's love strategy. Do they like to dress up, go out for cocktails and dance until dawn? Or do they enjoy a home-cooked meal, movie night and cuddling up? Love strategies are so interesting to learn about. One of my clients from many years ago had a love strategy that went like this: Girl comes up to him and whispers in his left ear. Yes, it can be that specific and simplistic.

When a relationship is not going well, changing the scenery will not change your behaviour. As you change on the inside, you will have the ability to benefit significantly more from the relationships you desire. The key to all successful relationships is how effortlessly you can suspend your incessant need to take from the relationship because you are trying to fill the emptiness inside. Replicating another person's strategies is about making deposits in the relationship bank.

Positive anchors

We looked at values and strategies above; the third area is about behavioural anchoring. It is one of those things that is so simple and powerful yet often it goes completely unnoticed and unused. Behavioural anchors are the foundation of human adaptability and survival. They play a major part within relationships as a trigger for negative or positive feelings, thoughts and actions. Anchors can be the make-or-break element of relationships. Each positive anchor adds funds to the relationship bank balance. Each negative anchor withdraws funds.

I first introduced you to the principle of anchoring and Pavlov's dogs back in Chapter 2. This psychosomatic phenomenon is pivotal in understanding how we learn, what we believe in and how we behave.

Imagine you see someone having an intensely happy experience (positive state), and your response is to smile and tip your head to the side (anchor). Simply put, every time you replicate the smile and tilt of your head, you'll trigger the person to remember either consciously or unconsciously the feelings of being intensely happy. The great news is you are then able to turn this feeling on for another person. If you did this by accident, that would be okay too.

Now for the not-so-great news. When you are in the presence of a person in a far less enjoyable emotional state, you might apply your unique stimulus, like having your face in theirs. That means every time they see your face, they will be consciously or unconsciously reminded of the less-than-empowering state. The unique stimulus could just be the sound of your voice. Do you remember the voice of your mother when she was not happy with you? Did she have a unique way of calling your name that meant, 'I'm in trouble now'?

I was watching a documentary many years ago with a focus on a couple who had a history of arguing, definitely on the verge of separation. As they sat in their chairs looking at each other, they started to discuss the issues that annoyed each other. In no time at all, they were yelling at each other and completely out of control. Heart rates racing, blood pressure climbing. As I watched, it was easy to notice that when one person looked sad, this look alone triggered anger in the other. The anger, on the other hand, seemed to trigger the look of sadness. Unfortunately for these two, it was like an emotional table tennis match of triggers and emotions. This dynamic was making huge withdrawals from their relationship bank account.

Now you could go out and set up a whole series of positive anchors and ignite them, or you could do something really radical: be observant. Learn what your partner or friend likes doing and do it. This may mean stepping out of your comfort zone, but it's well worth it. Spending time on things that are within your partner's or friend's top values will guarantee happy states to anchor upon.

CHAPTER 16

THE SEVEN HEARTS

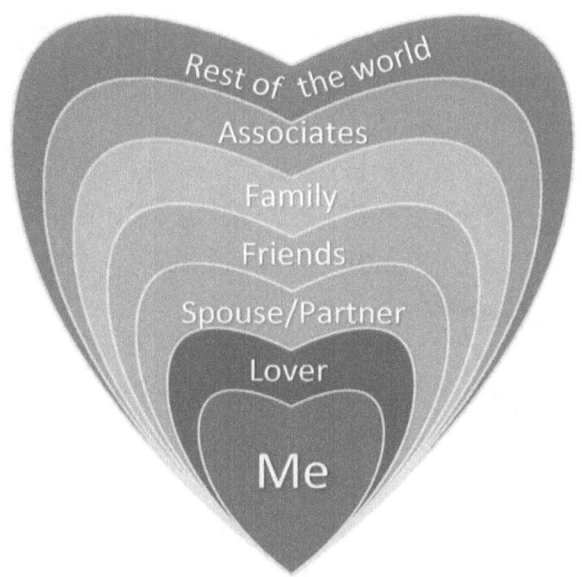

The seven hearts

Relationships can create feelings of love, joy, support and belonging, but they can also be a source of pain, frustration and suffering. The Seven Hearts method is about creating supportive, nurturing, inspiring, harmonious, fulfilling, deeper-bonded relationships.

In any of your relationships, are you …

- Constantly feeling let down
- Continually arguing about who is right and who is wrong
- Continually arguing over minor things

- Feeling betrayed
- Feeling you're always on different pages
- In an abusive relationship
- Feeling rejected or isolated
- Feeling abandoned or disconnected
- Blaming each other
- Constantly being misunderstood
- Feeling like you've got more skin in the relationship
- Observing your boundaries being crossed
- Feeling used or reciprocation is missing
- Feeling unvalued and unloved
- Feeling you can never do anything right
- Feeling the other person can never do anything right
- Feeling shamed, guilty, manipulated
- Feeling powerless

If you answered yes to any of the questions above, you're experiencing symptoms of relationship mismatching. The relationship type is not matched up with the person's deeds, attitude and behaviour. It's a simple case of a relationship type coding error. I have developed a method to help you unlock where the issues are occurring and teach you how to create wonderful, compatible and cherished connections, from today forward.

From Brisbane to Tokyo to Sydney

When I was a toddler in Brisbane in the 1960s, my parents left with me with people that didn't care for me. In fact, my parents abused me indirectly by leaving me with a family who allowed their children to beat me and traumatise me. I didn't feel I could tell my parents what was happening because I thought if I was no trouble to my parents, they would stop abandoning me. I thought if I was a good and obedient boy, they would keep me close and protect me. I recall as a four-year-old I would hide under the foster home with the dogs for fear of being beaten up. When you learn about the torture some children endure at the hands of their parents or other caregivers, you have to ask the question how can these adults give themselves the title of 'family'? Many would strip these abusers of such a title.

During the time I lived in Tokyo, Japan in the late 1980s, I was a student of a Shinto shrine of Tojinja. Tojinja was a priest who taught me the discipline and art of meditation. That year I spent a lot of time on my knees in silence. Tojinja also shared with me a fascinating relationship paradigm that he guided his churchgoers with when they were having relationship issues. The name he gave to it loosely translates in English to The Seven Hearts. I developed this paradigm into a method over a ten-year period. The method would be usable in Western cultures, specifically in my clinical sessions, and also as one of the most powerful personal development tools that I would go on to share with thousands of my students in my relationship courses in Sydney.

Within my classes I refer to the method as the Neuro Relationship Technique, but in this section I will be referring to the technique by its original name, The Seven Hearts, as I prefer that within the context of this book. I have used The Seven Hearts method now for over twenty-five years to help thousands of clients and students with their dysfunctional, abusive, disconnected or empty relationships. I'm going to share it here with you now so that you may plug it into your life to work its magic.

The seven hearts framework

The Seven Hearts framework explains how people organise relationships at a neurological level. We have a map in our brain that links behaviours of each of the significant people in our lives with generally one of six associated titles: lover; spouse/partner; family; friend; associate; rest of the world. When the default relationship title of a person and the behaviours of what you desire from a person with that title are mismatched, this is the formula for suffering, conflict and incompatibility.

The Seven Hearts method fundamentally tackles this incongruency by realigning the behaviours (and traits and actions) with the more appropriate relationship title of a person. What are the results of doing this realignment? Abuse is solved. Relationship problems that have brought on depression, feeling overwhelmed, drug-related issues, burn-out, anger and anxiety are instantly dissolved. Relationship issues don't have to be dramatic to be debilitating in your life. The issues you experience can simply be a mix of ongoing fighting, disappointment, feeling unloved, uncared for, infidelity, betrayal, confusion, sadness, guilt. By applying The Seven Hearts method, your relationships will be renovated, refreshed and revived. As a by-product you will form healthy connections that are deeper and more meaningful.

This method is not about abolishing every single problem you have in life with another person. The key here is you will now have the ability to problem solve easily and effortlessly because there is a natural alignment, affinity and commonality in the relationship. You are operating as a team.

Let's first take a dip into the most challenging relationship area. When it comes to relationship woes involving family, these are the trickiest of all to navigate. Why? Because the idea of family is loaded with these concepts: loyalty; honour; family always stick together; blood is thicker than water; manipulation through guilt and shame; conditional love; you can always lean on family; family is more important than anything else.

But what if your family is killing you? What if your family is removing your freedom to be you? What if your family is sabotaging your personal success? What if your family is draining your resources to the point of ill health and mental anguish? What if members of your family swing between abusive and loving? You may have some family members that fit into what your concept of how you expect family to be, and you may have some family members that are downright toxic and damaging to you. Just because they have historically been given the default title of family does not mean they can keep this title. They have to earn it and not by words but by deed (attitude, actions and behaviour) and traits (character, spirit, essence).

Many relationship issues exist when a significant person (or group) in your life has an attitude or a way of behaving that is out of sync with what you desire or expect. There is nothing wrong with the other person (or group) when they do not meet your expectations, as they are merely operating in accordance with their nature and that is something you cannot change. The issue you are having is in the way you have organised or categorised the important people in your life in your mind's filing system. You have a case of mismatching. We are about to embark on some simple yet profoundly life-changing reorganisation of the relationship filing cabinet that exists in your mental real estate.

The seven hearts method

Ready to play? It is most effective if you complete this method as a hands-on exercise. However, feel free to read along.

Set up (10 mins)

You need a pen, scissors, a measuring instrument (rule or tape measure), and four pieces of A4 or foolscap paper. From these four pieces of paper, create a total of sixteen equal-sized rectangular cards, that is, four cards from each piece of paper.

Sit at a table or a coffee table for this exercise. Place all sixteen blank cards in a pile in front of you.

Traits and Deeds

During the exercise you are going to encounter two words: traits and deeds. I'd like to clarify first what these are.

The term **TRAIT** means something you can observe in someone's **physical attributes, character, spirit or their essence.** Examples of this might be: kind, generous, funny, earthy, airy, practical, intelligent, cute, sexy, charming, tall, fit, thoughtful, caring, respectful, youthful, loving, warm, quick witted.

The term **DEED** means something which you can see or observe in someone's **action, behaviour or attitude.** Examples of this might be: takes the garbage out, makes me a cup of tea, goes hot ballooning with me, gives great kisses, makes me a birthday cake, is great in bed, touches my earlobe in the right way, looks after my cat when I'm away, listens to me without judgement, understands me, talks to my parents, is hardworking, laughs at my jokes, has fun on the weekends, reads the same type of books as I do.

Let's continue.

Discover your perfect relationship map

Using your imagination…

Enter the gaming room. Only you have access to this special room. This room is soundproof and completely secure and private. This room is invisible to the outside world. Your thoughts, feelings and conversations are kept within the four walls of this secret room. There are no other players. Any problems and angst around partners or spouse, family, friends and associates are left at the door. As you hear the door gently close behind you, allow a sense of peace and clarity to wash over you. Emotionally free, you walk forward. Double-check that you are relaxed, and any strong emotions are left outside the room.

Walk to the centre of the room to the table. Take up a seat in the chair with the word 'Me' on it.

Step 1: Relationship types

1. Pick up a blank card and write 'Family' in the centre.
2. Turn the card over and draw a line down the middle so you create two equal columns. On the left-hand column heading write 'Traits' and on the right-hand side column heading write 'Deeds'.
3. As quickly as you can, write down all the list of **traits** you desire a family member to have and then write a list of the **deeds** your perfect family member would do.

   ✓ It is crucial that you review your lists and check that you have written down the desired qualities of family and not what family members are currently exhibiting.

Step 2

Now place that card on the table in front of you with the word 'Family' facing down and the trait and deed lists you've just created facing up.

- ✓ Family

Step 3

Repeat Steps 1 and 2 for each of these three other relationship categories below. After completing each card, place on top of the completed pile, each with the category name facing down.

- ✓ Lover
- ✓ Partner/Spouse
- ✓ Friend

Step 4

1. Write the word 'Associate' on another blank card and on the reverse side write 'A person of service' at the top. Now draw two columns underneath. Column one has the heading 'Traits' and column two has the heading 'Deeds'.
2. Now write down the traits and the deeds of an associate. An associate is someone known to you who does not fit into any of the other relationship categories, but they are someone who you need or would like to be associated with.
3. Write 'Rest of the world' on another blank card and turn it over and write: 'Anyone that does not belong in any of the other relationship categories and does not matter to me personally'. Nothing else is needed to be written on this card unless you would like to elaborate on what 'Rest of the world' means to you.

- ✓ Associate
- ✓ Rest of the world

Now you will have a pile of six completed Relationship cards.

Step 5

Finally, you'll be working with the pile of ten blank cards left on the table. These are called your People cards.

1. Pick up one of the blank cards and write on it the name of the person that first comes to mind. This is usually the most important and significant person in your life.
2. Pick up another blank card and write the next most important or significant person in your life on it.
3. Continue this process until you have completed up to ten cards.
4. You can create as many People cards as you like. For now, create up to ten.

Step 6

Now for the moment of resolution.

1. Shuffle the Relationship cards and place them out in front of you with the label of the category still facing down.
2. Place each People card next to one of the six Relationship groups in front of you by matching this person with the traits and deeds they most closely fit with.
3. Notice I said traits and deeds and not title? This is crucial that you are matching the person with what is written in the traits and deeds column, or description. They may not have all the listed qualities of the group, but decide which group this person fits most closely with.

4. The person may fit with two groups e.g., lover and spouse or lover and friend. That is perfectly natural. Some of my students get quite excited by the prospect that their lover and spouse can be two different people!

Step 7

Now continue the matching of each of the People cards with each of the six groups.

Step 8

Now turn over each of your Relationship cards to display the title of the relationship category.

Step 9

Your perfect relationship map is now in front of you. This map is not conditional on blood relative status or living arrangement or care-giving relationship or any other contextual circumstances.

You will discover which of your top ten most important people in your life are matching in terms of their 'default title' and their traits and deeds. Sticking out like dogs' balls, you will see immediately where a person is mismatched in terms of their 'default title' and which group you have placed them with. It is here in the mismatches you will experience the most relationship conflict and dysfunction. The intended aim of The Seven Hearts method is all about relationship congruency by aligning title with traits and deeds.

What if your family group is empty? What if nobody important in your life has been placed with this group? Totally natural. It gives you the opportunity to fill that group with people who fulfil that criteria. The same goes for any of the other groups. You may not have anyone in the lover or spouse category. Now that you've completed your relationship map, you can clearly see your criteria for each relationship type, which is an enormous opportunity to assess whether your criteria are too narrow, or too wide. Where your attention and fine-tuning goes, people can flow.

One of my dear friends has such a beautiful, honest and gentle way of telling people they don't fit her friend criteria. There are many that want to be in her friend circle because she is so fun, generous and giving. She says to them, 'You wouldn't want to be my friend. My friend criteria are almost impossible to fulfil and it wouldn't be worth all the hard work for you.'

How your perfect relationship mind map operates in the real world

Once you have accepted and integrated your Relationship Mind Map (RMM), it will automatically run in the background. You will be overwriting the old map with your new, up-to-date map. The elegance of this is that nobody else needs to know if you have removed their 'default title' and moved them into a more appropriate relationship grouping. Say you have discovered that your mum no longer fits with the grouping family. She has the default title Mum, but in your RMM she may fit in the group 'friend' or 'associate' or 'rest of the world'. As you reorganise people in your RMM, the sense of calm and relief will be obvious and immediate because you are no longer wishing and wanting for someone to be someone they are not. What a relief for the other person too. Your desires are now matching reality. This releases you from the unrealistic expectations cycle and perpetuating disappointment for both sides. Internal or external conflict with another person will persist if you fail to acknowledge the true nature of yourself and the other person.

> **Treat a snake like a snake, no problem, but treat a snake like a rabbit and there will be trouble.**

Installing the RMM releases you neurologically from being trapped in an abusive relationship. It releases you from a loveless marriage and allows you to break free of the "til death do us part' sentiment. The constant feeling of being let down by someone you used to call friend whom you've discovered has the deeds and traits of an associate. The parent that had only loved you on the condition of this or that, is now in the rest of the world. The feelings of confusion turn into a feeling of belonging. The feeling of worthlessness turns into a feeling of value. Meaningful connections grow where the result is an improved sense of self-worth.

It will be natural for a grief process to follow, as with any change. There will be some emotional pain where you realise a person you care about deeply, for whom you have yearned to be in a specific role, is simply not geared up for it. Right now, you may have just realised the person you are married to does not behave like someone you would want to be married to.

What action do you take next in regard to the people who have default titles that do not match the deeds and traits of that group? This is your decision. There are three options. The first option is to change their title. The second option is to work on the deeds and traits to realign them with the title; this will require focus and work from both parties. The third is to take no action. Taking no action could mean continued suffering, but it can also lead to a more relaxed relationship because you are no longer expecting anything more from them. However, taking this third option will lead you away from being fulfilled in your life. Challenging emotions can be sparked up with any of the options, but you now have the clarity to choose a path.

By the way, your RMM is not permanently fixed. It develops and updates accordingly over time. People can and do change, including yourself. So, if someone today doesn't fit into any of your close relationship groups, in the future they may develop qualities that do eventually fit. Alternatively, you may mature with time or through experience your criteria evolve. Your criteria are held at an unconscious level. This is not something you tell yourself to change in a conscious manner.

Just because someone considers you as their friend, this does not mean they fall into your relationship category of 'friend'. This simply means that you have fulfilled their criteria. Meanwhile, they may have failed your criteria. Someone that considers you a daughter, you may not consider them satisfying your criteria of family or parent, but they are aligned more closely with the grouping of friend. Get the idea? Your RMM is unique to you and it will often not be in sync with how others consider you in their RMM. Deeper bonds form between two people when their RMMs are compatible.

Install your Relationship Mind Map

Are you ready to harmonise your relationships? Are you ready to relieve the undue suffering caused by unfulfilled expectations? Are you ready to stop the conflict and abuse? Are you ready to discover more meaning and depth in your relationships?

It's okay if you are not ready. Your decision about how you navigate life is one hundred per cent yours.

But if you are ready for transformation, let's go.

Installation

Have your Relationship cards to hand. If you completed these in your imagination, you'll be tapping into the imagined cards shortly.

Find a quiet place to sit in a comfortable chair. Create a bubble around you that is waterproof, bite proof and bomb proof. There is a tube that runs from the earth into the bottom of your bubble. There is another tube that runs from the sky into the top of your bubble. Both tubes connect into your heart space. This life tube brings you love, light, wisdom and anything else you need to survive, thrive and create.

As you focus on each breath out, you may notice how you feel more relaxed, or not. You may notice any areas of your body that may be less or more relaxed. Only you will know when you have connected your breath to your body, and this is the perfect time to open the door to change.

1. Pick up the first of your six Relationship cards and read the group name and ask your unconscious mind to locate where this group resides in your mind. Ask your mind to tag this area with a colour of your choosing.
2. Turn over the card and read the deeds and traits. Ask your mind to upload these into that area of your mind that you tagged.
3. Repeat Steps 1 and 2 for each of the other five relationship cards.

On completing the steps, you may choose to close your eyes if they feel heavy when blinking open and closed. After your eyes are closed, allow your RMM to integrate as you take three relaxed breaths. When you are ready to come back to the present after your integration is complete, count backwards from eight so that when you reach one, your eyes may open or choose to open when you are ready.

What to expect and what's next?

At the beginning of this chapter, I listed a whole range of relationship-related issues that can occur when there is a mismatch of a person's qualities to their default title. These issues, if not completely, will largely dissolve, depending on how well you've matched the significant people in your life to each relationship type.

You may notice in the future when you interact with the people you have moved from the more intimate or close circle groups to the more distant relationship groups, that they are no longer triggering you. They may seem confused as to why your old buttons are not firing anymore. There will be some high emotions where there was once an unhealthy attachment or co-dependency, and each party may experience grief, anger, sadness. These feelings will pass.

If you have discovered that someone no longer fits with their default title, you can choose to work together to close the gaps. We can all evolve if we want to and if we see value in that change. Particularly when it comes to deeds, someone can potentially learn how to do them for another with a small amount of effort and care. Sure, if you have deal-breaker deeds that the other party just cannot perform because it is against their ethics or morals, then this is good to identify sooner rather than later. For identifying and resolving other relationship issues, refer back to Chapter 15's section entitled Rich Relationships.

The outcome of The Seven Hearts method is not reducing the people you have in your life, rather it's about defining how you relate to them in a new dynamic if the old dynamic wasn't working. Your incompatibilities are converted into compatibilities once you have organised who sits where on your Seven Hearts map.

A healthy, successful relationship is one that holds up during a stormy period. It's easy being around someone during the smooth sailing periods. The real test of relationship strength is riding the ups and downs with compassion, resourcefulness and forgiveness.

CHAPTER 17

IT'S ALL ABOUT YOU

It's all about you

Problems, challenges and issues in life can be traced back to a single relationship issue. It's the relationship you have with yourself. The quality of your relationships is a direct reflection of the quality of the relationship you have with yourself. The quality of your life is a direct reflection of the level of respect and love you have cultivated for yourself.

Do you respect yourself? How do you talk to yourself? Do you have a harsh inner critic? How well do you look after yourself? How do you nurture your body, your mind, your spirit? Do you take responsibility for your actions and choices?

With self-love, nobody can manipulate you by dangling the promise of acceptance or love in front of you. Love and self-acceptance are only found within you. Those on the outside are mirrors of you. And you are a mirror to them.

How we get on in life is driven by our perceptions, societal conditioning, your body health, your choices. There is no good or bad, right or wrong. Your practise is to observe yourself. Observing the observer is your most powerful tool in your toolbox. Any time you are troubled, challenged or stuck, this is your first tool to pick up to gain an objective view of the situation before deciding on your path of action. Self-awareness is your superpower.

When we improve our connection with ourselves, everything else falls into place. Your unconscious mind and body are already in your favour and working in accordance with the blueprint of your whole and natural health and true happiness. Continuing to look outside yourself to solve a puzzle that originates from within you can lead to deep sadness, anxiety, depression, helplessness.

The more you connect with your authentic, divine, sacred self, the more you will connect with others who are also authentic and real.

The love and respect you cultivate for yourself will ripple out into the world. This is the path to world peace.

> **Mastering others is strength.**
> **Mastering yourself is true power.**
> **—Lao Tzu**

Malise Banks, one of my beautiful heart-centred graduate students will guide you in an Inner Child Meditation as a spirit-lifting conclusion to this part of the book. Malise is a trainer, coach and spiritual guidance counsellor with over ten years of experience in the field of personal empowerment and spiritual growth.

Your inner child
By Malise Banks

> *It is the relationship we have with ourselves that is the greatest influence on the success of our relationships with others. That's why a powerful meditation has been included in the following pages, with the focus on healing the first aspect of you that came into this*

world, that of your Inner Child. In this meditation we radically shift your trajectory by transforming any unresolved needs you missed out on as a child, which may still be wreaking havoc on your relationship with yourself and others today.

Your Inner Child represents innocence, wonder, joy, sensitivity and playfulness, however, it also holds your accumulated childhood hurts, traumas, fears and anger. As adults we often suppress these unmet needs despite their constant nagging to try and control our ever-present reality. It's interesting to note that many adults are actually led by their emotionally wounded Inner Child. This does not bode well for healthy relationships.

The most powerful and divine essence of you is known as your Higher Self. This is your true self, the part that remains eternal, omnipotent, conscious and intelligent. You can turn to your Higher Self for the wisdom, direction and strength that comes direct from Source. Meditation opens the communication with your Inner Child and Higher Self.

Meditation is a wonderful way to return harmony to your mind, body and spirit, and in turn, heal your relationship with yourself and others. Meditation entails spending time in the only space that is real – the present moment. Our society has taught us to live in the past and the future. Did you know that not even one single negative emotion can live in the present moment? This is because time and space stop here. This is the place where you connect to something that is greater than you, and where you find peace.

With regular meditation, everything stops, and the background buzz disappears. You will experience longer and longer periods of bliss during your practice of being present. Most of all, you will see your life transform before your eyes. Your burdens, issues and challenges will work themselves out, to be replaced with flow. Your body will return to its optimum state and your mind will be *working with you, the way it was designed to. Perhaps for the first time, you will feel connected, with yourself and others.*

Another transformative aspect of meditation is that you are intentionally spending time in a higher vibration. Not only does this mean you are healing your body right down to a cellular level, but you are also attracting similar frequencies, building up the strength of your good intentions for your life. As Plato said all those years ago, 'Like attracts like', and meditation is a way of concentrating loving vibrations that will naturally sync with those around you. Imagine the loving relationships you are attracting when you spend regular time in higher vibrations.

The following meditation is a powerful quantum healing process to bring harmony to your Inner Child.

You might like to record your voice reading this script and play this back to yourself. Alternatively, visit www.gdlife.co/bookfreebies for your complementary meditation guidance.

Inner child meditation

Find a quiet space and a comfortable seat to sit in.

> *Taking several deep breaths…*
> *Make yourself comfortable…*
> *Place your feet flat on the floor…*
> *Gently allow your eyelids to close…*
> *And just begin to allow yourself to relax…*
> *Letting all your cares and worries go…*
> *And at this moment in time…*
> *Nothing matters…*

Ever since you were born, you've learned and experienced something each and every moment of your life. Today is another one of these special moments.

Today you are going to travel to a unified place where you will see the strands of time and space dissolve ... Where you will meet the innocent essence of you.

In your mind's eye, you look up slowly and see that you are surrounded by a mighty wall of golden white light, streaming in all directions; a living, liquid light that envelops you like a giant golden bubble.

Within this protective bubble, you notice the heightened feelings of love as you feel a steady stream of light pouring upon you, in you and through you.

You are aware of a deep knowing that this sphere of protective light comes from the higher realms and is secure and unconquerable and whose origins are from pure, unconditional love. Dark matter cannot make its way past the barriers of this golden bubble. Nothing can get in but love, light and air. You know you are safe, secure and content.

You look up and notice there is an opening in the bubble above your head that comes from the heavens, providing you with an endless supply of love, light and air. As this steady stream falls upon you, you feel your body becoming lighter, and you feel every cell in your body returning to a harmonic order, the way it was intended. You can feel the swish of this stream of love, light and air dissolving any energetic blocks.

You spend some time basking in this magical place, free of time and space. Connecting with your sacred heart space, just allowing the flow of love to stream upon you, in you and through you.

Breathing it all in, noticing that each exhale lightens your energy, dissolving any density, releasing the artificial controls you were holding on to, freeing you to bask in the love from your heart. You know there is a bigger picture in place and that you no longer need to hold on to any worries.

You feel a surge of faith and trust as you witness yourself fully surrendering to love. Waves of peace flow through you as you more fully align with your heart in this moment.

You look down and notice there is someone else here with you now, standing at your feet. It is a little child. You look closer and realise this child is you.

You gaze down in awe as you witness the purity and innocence of your Younger Self.

You sense the wonder, joy, playfulness and sensitivity of this precious being at your feet. Your Younger Self is looking up to you, wondering what to do ... a trusting innocence sparkles in your Younger Self's eye.

You bend down to meet your Younger Self and look deeply into your eyes. Your Younger Self is uncertain and clearly needs you. You feel your heart opening as you take your Younger Self's hand.

In soft and gentle words, you whisper, 'I am here to protect you. You are no longer alone in this realm or any other realm in time and space. I am here to take charge, to bring things into harmony and to restore love in your life where it was missed.

'I am sorry for some of the things I neglected to do to nurture you. I'm sorry I didn't have the time, or the knowledge or resources to give you exactly what you needed.

'I have come here to look after you. You did the best you could at the time, acting in a certain way for a good reason, but that reason is no longer needed because you are loved and accepted.'

You bend down, pick up and hold your Younger Self close to you.

Look deeply into your Younger Self's eyes and ask, 'What is it that you need? What is it that you missed receiving, knowing, feeling?' Give your Younger Self time to answer, then reply, 'I give all of your heart's desires to you now.'

You witness a rainbow wave of colours flow through your heart to your Younger Self and notice your Younger Self's smile become wider and wider.

'Is there anything else that you need?'

Again, wait for an answer, then...

'I give you these things now that you missed and that have always been your birthright.'

Vivid reds, oranges, greens, blues and purples stream through your heart and into your Younger Self.

'I am here to make sure you know that every single part of you is loved, that no part is left out. Each part is loved and appreciated.'

Watch as the rainbow of harmonic resonance swirls upon, in and through your Younger Self, harmonising right down to a cellular level.

You notice that the miraculous healing taking place for this precious child is simultaneously healing you too. These brilliant rainbow energies are transforming your mind, body and spirit in the now, just as they are healing on a quantum level across all time and space.

'I will always be here to nurture, care and love you. I will always listen to you in the future. Your desires and feelings matter. From now on, every minute of every day I will be there to support, play with, guide and understand you. I will provide these things so that you will grow up to be strong and secure in yourself.'

Today a declaration of restoration and healing has been made for you that echoes throughout the planes of time and space for eternity. Your Younger Self is now a strong, secure and a loving adult in the next chapters of life.

Your Younger Self now knows their sacred birthright and their highest potential is nurtured and protected beyond time and space.

Before you put your Younger Self down, embrace them lovingly, a lasting reminder that they are loved ... and then gently allow your Younger Self to step down to the floor of the golden bubble.

Just before you prepare to return to your now moment in time, notice your Higher Self standing there with you. Your Higher Self has the virtues of the Divine and lovingly whispers these Divine traits in your ear, to remind you of who you really are. Listen carefully for the words that describe your Divine qualities. Perhaps you are a loving, powerful, caring and nurturing presence … or intelligent, adaptable and creative … or compassionate, strong and forgiving. Just allow your Higher Self to impart these truths to you now.

Notice how you feel a strong sense of self-worth, self-acceptance and self-love in this moment. These honoured qualities have been returned to their rightful place in your heart, on this quantum healing journey today.

Realise that all of these things come from within you. You are a mighty warrior, worthy of love, worthy of peace, worthy of knowing, deep from within your heart, that you are a sacred being of love. Feel your hearts beat in unison, a unified rhythm between you, your Inner Child and your Higher Self.

Now, when you are ready, slowly come back to the present and open your eyes.

OUTRO

What have you discovered about yourself on this short journey we have taken together? How has your self-awareness expanded? What relationship enrichments did you create? Do you find yourself equipped with more compassion for yourself and others? Did you collect a range of communication tools to put in your evergreen toolkit for living a fulfilling life? My desire for you is that your moments of richness flow into your bank of the good life.

My mission is to bring heaven to earth. If just one person breathes easier because of my existence, I have done my job. Twenty years ago when Tojinja the Japanese priest who was my spiritual mentor told me I was one of twelve and my life would not be my own, I filed this idea away in my memory banks. On recently contemplating his praise or curse, depending how I look at it, I feel I now understand what he intended. He considered my qualities analogous to one of the twelve apostles that could teach humanity about bringing heaven to earth. He observed my potential to connect with my divine purpose to heal, and that if I wandered off my healer path, I'd be guided back to it with invisible force. I am deeply grateful to Tojinja for holding so much faith in me.

When each one of us sets out to create peace within ourselves, this is all that is needed to bring peace upon humanity. Inner peace is achieved when each part of you reconciles, with the fragmented parts of your mind and body singing the same song, walking the same path, being in love. The practise of compassion for others is acknowledging their why and their what, no matter how different it is to your way. You acknowledge the wonderful differences, but you also recognise we are all the same.

Prophetically, exactly four weeks before Robb Whitewood suddenly and unexpectedly passed away on the thirtieth of March 2017, he posted the following article online.

Life is life

Life is life, nothing more; it promises nothing and sometimes is totally unexpected. The quest for all of us is to make some sense out of our existence. Are we immortal beings that live through eternity, moving from one body to another, or do we just vanish into nothingness at the point of our demise? Are we to live for the future, preparing for a point in time where everything will be better one day? Do we dwell in the past, attempting to understand the relationships, decisions and events that brought us to this moment? The fundamental truth of all of this is no-one knows. Everyone is creating stories in an attempt to make sense of it all. You could say this is pessimistic, or is it just realistic? What I do know is that today is all there is; tomorrow is just a dream and that yesterday has gone. The perfection of a day lived well is the thing that creates life. Governments, churches, schools, employers and parents all fighting for a place in your mind to insert their stories so that you will give up a little or all of your today for them. In this way, you become a slave to the stories we tell ourselves. The only question you have to ask is, 'Am I a slave to my story or is it someone else's story that is controlling my life?'

Embracing mortality

For many, mortality is the most disturbing truth about life. It is the one truth that most of us do our absolute best to ignore, hide and overall, deny.

We are all going to die. Yes, I said it. Die.

Life is a game that has one inevitable and unavoidable outcome. Statistically speaking, it is a game that no-one gets out of alive. Now having been hit with this sobering fact, rejoice. When you live in denial and pretend death is an event that just happens to other people but never to you, you will start to live what I call a 'shadow life'. When you turn your eyes away from the inevitability, you do so at the cost of missing all the other things that exist.

Remember when you fear a thing or deny a thing, the thing denied will end up controlling you. It will end up stealing resources, taking the most precious of all things: in this case, your quality of life. Remember a second wasted on the fear of death is a second that can never be recovered. It is lost forever. Denial of death lets you pretend that you will live forever, which gives you permission to not do things in the moment, as mistakenly you think there is all the time in the world.

> **The most vital attitude to mastering the good life lies in embracing your mortality.**

I would like to conclude with some words by Tania Browitt, who believes that the human spirit has vast potential and is always seeking ways to grow. As a practitioner, Tania has a unique ability to empathise and bring an alchemy of change to people's lives with her coaching and modalities.

Masks, desires, pulsions and drivers
By Tania Browitt

Once we stop and reconcile all the disparate parts of self that are positioned along our perceived timeline, we start an energy-reclamation process and transcend the mystery of all levels of our light bodies.

Our pure existence is a vibration code that is beyond the physical and is the surgence of the invisible self – near and far. We as humans stage a visual construction and deconstruction of subjectivity. We transition from entrapment in culturally and religiously imprinted beliefs to a liberation through self-awareness of the coded, socially constructed self.

I believe as human beings, we are what we are on the basis of something that we experience as missing, having a desire for the impossible suture: the eternal return to nature or the mother.

The mask is not a guise of our reality but a substitute for the void beneath us all. The mask of socially constructed subjectivity is a shield-like artifice that enables the creation of an identity by purporting to cover up something really there, hidden under the play of surfaces; something waiting to be bestowed or unearthed. The engagement of the mask is often not to hide the real person underneath, rather it functions as a substitute for the shock discovery of the nothingness behind it, the void in its raw exposure. Is it too much to bear?

Our freedom, then, lies in the consciousness of this process and a chance to mould a subjectivity more in tune with our own pulsions, desires and drivers, rather than the one partially constructed for us by the existing socio-cultural world we inhabit.

We can imagine a universe beyond the surface of our perceptions.

Working with neurology and physiology is the beginning, unfolding in sacred geometry of the vibratory world of quantum mechanics is to signal us in new ways, finding what is essential, what is most meaningful, into liberation, bliss and freedom.

I emerged from trauma and hiding into a world of infinite possibilities and mastered my good life effectively, visibly, with great influence and inspiration from all around me.

I learnt from Robb that you can run, but you can't hide. Finally, I could trust the vehicle: Me.

The day you know you are a tree and water at the same time, you will have found home. —Allison Low

ACKNOWLEDGMENTS

Without our parents we would not have been inspired to write this book. Our parents' support and loving pressure helped shape our path and determination. Thank you to the late Gordon Whitewood, the late Blanche Whitewood, Norman Low and Ann Low. A special mention goes to Allison's three brothers, Christopher Low, Jason Low and Brenden Low, who tackled, teased, stretched and loved her. Without them she would be a mouse.

Allison is deeply grateful to her partner, Daniel Menne, who has supported her emotionally through some turbulent times. Without him, this book would not have existed. He held the space for Allison whilst she was consumed by her late husband's work over a three-year period. An incredible, selfless act.

We are deeply grateful to each and every member of the team that has helped and supported us to bring this book into reality.

Editor
Bryony Sutherland

Manuscript Support
Adelaide Damoah, Malise Banks, Anna Dernham, Helen Semmens, Marie Barrett, Daniel Menne.

Book Writing Guidance
Mediumship and spiritual guidance: Rebecca Mayhew
Book Coach: Nicole Johnston

Graphics
Cover Concept: Allison Low
Cover Design: The Scaly Merchant
Sketch Artist: Beverley Willson
Electronic Graphic Art Support: Marie-Line Villers
Book Design: Ekow Addai

Contributors
Maike Sundmacher, Malise Banks, Jane Nash, Sukie Baxter, Tania Browitt

Music that inspired the flow of writing
Estas Tonnes, *Internal Flight*

Robb's mentors and influencers:
Erle Montaigue, Alex Ivanoff, Dr Richard Bandler, Dr John Grinder, Dr Willie Monteiro, Wyatt Woodsmall, Quentin Strauli, Robert Dilts, Marvin Oka, Dan Millman, Dr Wayne Dyer, Judith DeLozier, Winnie-the-Pooh, and many more…

Allison's mentors and influencers:
Robb Whitewood, Osho, Allan Wilson Watts, Thich Nhat Hahn, Dr Richard Bandler, Tara Brach, Dr Tom Cowan, Dr Zach Bush, Leo Bursa, Teal Swan, The School of Life, Vandana Shiva and many more…

ACKNOWLEDGMENTS

To our precious friends, family, students, clients and associates who made financial contributions to assist in the publishing of this book (listed in alphabetic order by first name).

Adriano Raiola
Alana Spinks
Alexey Prokopenko
Alton Chan
Amy Spain
Andrew Cranwell
Andrew Gowans
Andrew Watt
Angela McCloy
Angelique Jiang
Angelique Low
Ann Low
Annette Wyllie
Barbara Ukmar
Belinda Stewart
Bhawani Singh
Cathy Newman
Chris Canty
Christian de Stoop
Christopher Luke
Chrystal Scadding
Daniel Menne
David Brooks-Horn
Deane Scadding
Dennis O'Brien
Edwina Tam
Eleen Yaw

Fernando Moreno
Genevieve Stewart
Gladys Noszkowski
Glenn Sutton
Ibrahim Hanania
Jamii Hart
Jane Nash
Jasmine Low
Jason Low
Jenny McFadden
Jenny Twaddle
Joe Saba
Johanna Watt
John Clarke
Julie Sutton
Julie-Anne Morgan
Kate Robinson
Kim Creef
Kirilly Middleton
Lea Clarke
Lindy Hamid
Ling Low
Lisa Armstrong
Lorraine Khouri
Louise Luke
Lucy Watt
Lyndell Dempsey

Madeleine Sheldon
Maria Saladino
Matthew Luke
Michael Dempsey
Michael Gee Lewis
Miriam Howard
Nafsika Divis
Neil Nash
Neysa King
Nikita Panikar
Niro Dayalan
Norma Beitinger
Norman Low
Pamela Darby-Mann
PJ Shepherd
Rebecca Glissan
Rhonda Watt
Rob McAdam
Robert Massat
Robert Talevski
Sanja Ademovic
Sarah Gowans
Scott Macdonald
Sergey Tsyplakov
Steven Morgan
Strategy, Planning and Performance Team, The University of Newcastle
Toni Payne
Tricia Shannon
Trisha Seeto
Tristan Curry
Warren Seeto
Werner Menne
Yu Dan Shi

LAST WORDS FROM THE AUTHORS

Allison Low

I've reached a point in my life where I find it impossible to describe who and what I am. My accomplishments, where I was born, where I have lived and the vast experiences I have had, will fall short of how I'd like to be regarded. My mission is to be a light for others where there was once dark. My intention is to be an activator for others, not drive a bus of passengers. I seek to push my own boundaries and welcome fears so that I can overcome them, for life is to be experienced as expansively as my imagination. My wish for humanity is that we recognise that we are one and the same magical force.

Robb Whitewood (1960 - 2017)

Like Allison, I prefer not to list out my certifications and my expansive experience in life; rather I'd like to share a bit about myself. I didn't find love until I was forty-five years old. I just didn't love myself enough before then to feel truly loved. Unlike Allison, my childhood was full of abandonment and trauma. I pay homage to that time, for without it, this book would not have been written. I would not otherwise have needed to solve my own pain and in doing so gathered the wisdom to help others to do the same. I'd often jest that if I didn't choose the healer path, I'd either be in jail or dead by the age of twenty-five. I've been truly fortunate to have been loved by so many in my later years, which has certainly filled me up to share the love around.

I feel like I've lived three lifetimes and if I died tomorrow, I'd have no regrets because I have had a full and rich life. The most wonderful thing in my life is seeing the lights go on in my students' minds each time I teach. It is what fulfils me. My wish for you is that you discover what your path is, get on it and enjoy the ride, right now.

SUGGESTED READING AND VIEWING

Reading

A Course in Miracles by Helen Schucman

Accessing the Healing Power of the Vagus Nerve by Stanley Rosenberg

Frogs Into Princes: Introduction to Neuro Linguistic Programming by Richard Bandler and John Grinder

Man's Search for Ultimate Meaning by Viktor E Frankl

Science and Sanity by Alfred Korzybski

Tao Te Ching by Lao Tzu, translated by Stephen Mitchell

The Body Keeps Score: Brain, Mind, And Body in the Healing of Trauma by Bessel van der Kolk, M.D.

The Holographic Universe: The Revolutionary Theory of Reality by Michael Talbot

The I Ching, or Book of Changes by Hellmut Wilhelm & Cary F Baynes

The Life You Were Born to Live: A Guide to Finding Your Purpose by Dan Milman

The 7 Habits of Highly Effective People by Stephen R Covey, Sean Covey, et al.

The Tao of Pooh and the Te of Piglet: The principles of Taoism Demonstrated by Winnie-the-Pooh and Piglet by Benjamin Hoff

Way of the Peaceful Warrior by Dan Milman

Your Erroneous Zones by Wayne Dyer

Viewing

Being There (1979)
Finding Joe
Harvey (1950)
I am Fishead
Star Wars: Return of the Jedi
The Matrix
The Razor's Edge (1946)
What the Bleep!? Down the Rabbit Hole

ONLINE RESOURCE LINKS

Contact details for all contributors of this book are detailed on our website: http://www.gdlife.co/booklinks

Your book freebies: http://www.gdlife.co/bookfreebies

ROBB'S BIO

Robb Whitewood founded Dynamic Mind Works in 1999, with a vision of improving life for hundreds of thousands of individuals around the world. Robb was a rare combination of a trainer, motivator, and entertainer. His wisdom and near-magical healing abilities led his students to name him "Earth Angel".

Born to international entertainers in Brisbane, Australia in 1960, Robb had travelled to many parts of the world by the age of seven. Throughout his life, Robb had a strong affinity with both Chinese and Japanese cultures, practising martial arts and following Taoist philosophy. His mastery in martial arts afforded him work for several years as a stunt actor in TV commercials, movies, and TV shows.

From the age of fifteen, Robb studied and practised Chinese Medicine, later becoming a highly skilled and qualified Acupuncturist and Diagnostician.

Robb became a Master Trainer in NLP and Hypnosis; he was also a highly sort after clinician from the 1990's right up until his unexpected passing in 2017.

ALLISON'S BIO

A LLISON LOW WAS BORN in Sydney, Australia to hard working good citizen parents. As a Eurasian in the early 70's growing up in country NSW it both grounded and tested her resilience to overcome discrimination. Over the past 25 years Allison has travelled to over forty countries and has lived in both England and Germany for several years.

Allison has a bachelor's degree in science and honours degree in psychology. She has worked as an analyst programmer for most of her career in over seventeen multi-national companies. In parallel to studying and working in the world of logic, she has trained in remedial massage, EFT, NLP, Hypnosis and has worked concurrently as a therapist in a wide range of healing modalities. Most importantly, today her intense focus is on energy (frequency) medicine, where she believes the future of healing lies.

Her mission is to help heal the world by empowering each individual to connect with their source of peace and creativity and live in harmony with their community and nature.

www.ingramcontent.com/pod-product-compliance
Lightning Source LLC
Chambersburg PA
CBHW022041290426
44109CB00014B/938